WAGON GIRL

WAGON GIRL

by

ELEANOR WATKINS

KINGSWAY PUBLICATIONS
EASTBOURNE

Paperback edition 1982

ISBN 0 86065 178 9

Printed in Great Britain for
KINGSWAY PUBLICATIONS LTD
Lottbridge Drove, Eastbourne, E. Sussex BN23 6NT by
Fakenham Press Limited, Fakenham, Norfolk

CONTENTS

CHAPTER ONE

THE LAST DAY OF SCHOOL

Ruth had finished the verse which her class had been set to copy long before the others. She looked at it, written somewhat untidily on her slate, but with every word spelt correctly. It was all about the value of good behaviour, and she thought it was a very silly verse, but then Miss Thatcher was fond of silly verses of that sort.

Ruth sighed and fidgeted, and her slate pencil fell with a clatter to the floor. Immediately Miss Thatcher's keen grey eyes were upon her, together with the eyes of most of Ruth's classmates.

"Ruth Carey! Kindly attend to your work!" rapped the stern voice which could cause even the biggest boys to quail.

"I've finished, please ma'am," said Ruth meekly, retrieving her pencil.

"Then fold your hands and sit quietly," said the teacher.

Ruth folded her hands on her slate and sat, wishing that the lesson, and the school day, would end. She knew that Mary Rebecca in her seat at the back of the room was looking disapprovingly at her from behind, and could imagine the lecture she would no doubt receive on the way home. "Oh, Ruth, must you do this—or that—or speak rudely to Miss Thatcher—or play with rough boys—or trail your dress in the mud——" The list was endless.

Ruth sighed and glowered, then her eye was caught by her nine-year-old cousin David, two years younger than herself and so a bench or two in front of her, who turned slightly and gave her his quick, cheeky grin. Ruth grinned back; no-one could remain gloomy long in sight of David's cheerful, freckled face.

She was wondering whether she and David would have time to go to their tree-house after supper that evening, when suddenly Miss Thatcher cleared her throat and announced that the lesson was at an end and school dismissed for the afternoon. Immediately there was a great rustling of dresses and clattering of slates, followed by the shuffling of feet and rattling of lunch pails as the children left the school-house. Each one paused to wish good afternoon to Miss Thatcher on his or her way out.

To Ruth's surprise, the teacher called, "Just a minute, Ruth," as she passed, and motioned her to stand beside the big desk.

For a moment Ruth searched her mind for her latest crime in need of punishment, and then she saw that Mary Rebecca, David and a little group of other farmers' children were also standing there. Then realisation dawned. These were the pioneers' children, and today was the last day at school for all of them.

Miss Thatcher was shaking hands with each of them, speaking a few kind words, and giving each a pretty little bookmark text to keep. To Ruth's dismay she saw that all the children were giving the teacher a farewell present in return—a neatly hemmed handkerchief, or a pen-wiper, or some such thing. Mary Rebecca had an elaborate sampler which she had spent hours embroidering with roses and forget-me-nots and a verse which said, 'When this you see, remember me.' Underneath was her name, Mary Rebecca Carey, her age, thirteen years, and the date, late April in the early eighteen-sixties, all done in cross-stitch. Even

David had a big rosy apple as his offering. Some recently uttered but only vaguely remembered words of Mary Rebecca's came into Ruth's mind. "Now, Ruth, don't forget to have something nice to give Miss Thatcher on our last day." But of course she had forgotten, and now she had nothing to give!

She waited last in the line, wondering what to do. Miss Thatcher's usually stern face was smiling kindly, her tone was gentle; she seemed almost sorry to be seeing the last of some of her pupils. How Ruth wished she had taken notice of Mary Rebecca for once and had something to offer her teacher. Then it was her turn, and Miss Thatcher paused a little before taking Ruth's hand.

"Well, Ruth," she said a little wryly, "we haven't always seen eye to eye, have we?"

Ruth shook her head, suddenly ashamed of the many times she had made trouble for the teacher, with her madcap ways. But Miss Thatcher was continuing in the kindest of tones:

"However, I know things haven't always been easy for you. But you're a bright, intelligent girl with, I believe, the makings of a fine woman. Be sure you don't neglect those fine qualities which are deep down inside you." She handed Ruth the last little text, and shook hands with the girl.

A lump rose in Ruth's throat. No-one had ever before told her that she had fine qualities. How she wished she had a gift to offer in exchange for those kind words!

Suddenly she was conscious of a hard lump in the pocket of her pinafore. She had forgotten that she had smuggled her most treasured possession to school that morning—a neat, small catapult made by her cousin John especially for her. She and David had intended getting in some target practice on the way home. Well, it was a beautiful catapult and the best thing she had. Ruth quickly put her hand into her pocket, drew out the catapult, and presented it to Miss Thatcher.

"It's a real good one—best hickory wood," she explained.

For a moment the teacher's face was a study of astonishment, then a twinkle appeared in her grey eyes. "Thank you—I shall treasure it," she said gravely, and leaning forward she kissed Ruth quickly on the cheek.

Ruth was conscious of the outraged expression on Mary Rebecca's face as they left the school-house and took the path through the woods which led home. Her cousin's cheeks were red and her mouth pursed up in a tight line.

"Well, Ruth Carey!" she said as soon as they were out of earshot of the others. "I declare I've never been so mortified in all my life. Whatever made you give Miss Thatcher a—a catapult! Of all things!"

Ruth held her copper-coloured head high, unrepentant. "I don't care. I hadn't anything else to give. Anyway, she liked it, so there!"

Mary Rebecca said nothing, but her cheeks grew redder and her mouth pursed up even tighter. The lunch pail swung crossly to and fro as she walked. David was a little ahead, shuffling his bare feet in the grass, and he turned and winked at Ruth. "It'll come in handy for scaring the birds off her cherries," he said.

A little picture of stern Miss Thatcher, complete with night-cap, leaning out of her bedroom window and taking pot-shots at a plump blackbird on her cherry-tree, popped into Ruth's mind. She exploded with laughter and laughed until she had a stitch and

Ruth's Aunt Susanna was busy at the big iron cook-stove in the corner of the room, from which savoury smells were issuing. Apart from the stove, chairs and table, the room was bare. Everything else was either sold or packed up ready for the big trip West.

Aunt Susanna was of medium height, on the plump side, with brown hair just beginning to show a few grey streaks. She had a bustling, no-nonsense manner and, like her older daughter, could be a trifle fussy, but underneath there was a heart of pure gold. Ruth's Uncle Seth sat in his big chair reading the paper, his long legs stretched out in front of him and his bushy, black beard resting on his chest. Near his feet the twins, two-and-a-half years old and golden-haired, were playing quietly with their home-made building blocks.

"My, what long faces," remarked Aunt Susanna as the children came in. "Are you all so sorry to see the last of school, then?"

"Not me," declared David cheerfully. He helped himself to a crumb of gingerbread from a pan cooling by the stove, earning himself a sharp rap across the knuckles from his mother's wooden spoon. Ruth and Mary Rebecca hung up their bonnets, washed their hands at the basin near the door, and began to set the table. John came in from the yard, the oldest of the Carey family, sixteen years old, dark-haired and already nearly six feet tall and as broad-shouldered as a man. He washed his hands and paused on his way to the table to tweak the apron strings of the two girls. Mary Rebecca frowned, but Ruth smiled at him adoringly. How she wished she was as old as John, and a boy! Then she could work outdoors and ride and shoot instead of there being the endless sewing and cooking and housework which Aunt Susanna took such pains to try to teach her.

Supper was soon ready and the whole family gathered round the table. Uncle Seth put away his newspaper, folded it carefully, and took his place at the head of the table. Aunt Susanna sat at the other end, handy to the stove, with the twins tied into high chairs on either side of her. Ruth, sniffing hungrily, took her place beside Mary Rebecca, opposite the two boys. A year ago she would have piled her plate greedily and begun to eat at once, but now she remembered to bow her head demurely and wait while Uncle Seth asked a blessing. And certainly the fried ham, the mashed potatoes and turnips and gravy, the apple-pie and gingerbread tasted no worse for the delay.

"Well," remarked Uncle Seth when everyone had been served, "I've seen William Robertson this afternoon, and he's managed to find a buyer for his homestead at last. It looks as though we'll be starting on Monday morning for sure."

These words, spoken in Uncle Seth's deep, rumbling tones which went so well with his burly six-feet-three-inch frame, sent a little thrill of excitement round the table. They had known they were to set out in the next week or so, but Monday—that was even sooner than they had expected.

"Hooray!" chirped David through a mouthful of fried ham and turnip. He was not really allowed to speak at the table, but for once his parents let it pass. To him the forthcoming journey West was the greatest lark that had happened in his short life.

"Hooray!" echoed Daniel, the boy twin.

Deborah, the girl twin, banged her spoon on the table and beamed at her brothers.

The twins were too young to understand what was happening, but they could sense the excitement of the others.

Ruth looked around at the rest of the family. Aunt Susanna's face had its usual expression of brisk cheerfulness as she helped Daniel to load his spoon with mashed potato and gravy. Ruth knew that at first she had been unwilling to uproot the family from their busy, secure life here and take them across the country into a strange, new land. She had worried about the long journey with its possible perils: wolves, hostile Indians, illness, hardship. But she was a brave, loyal wife who would follow her husband to the ends of the earth if need be. Before long she had agreed to sell the farm and join the next wagon train, and ever since she had busily and cheerfully been planning for the trip.

Mary Rebecca had her usual calm, slightly superior look. She had not wanted to leave home at all, and had shed many secret tears over going away from her friends, her school, her home. But she had long since sensibly decided to make the best of it.

John's face shone with the prospect of getting on the move at last. He was eager for a new land, new adventures, and was not afraid of hardship and danger. What was good enough for his father was good enough for him!

As for Ruth herself, she felt she could hardly wait to begin. The moment's regret she had felt earlier was forgotten, and she wondered how she would ever get through the two long days before they could start. She had eagerly drunk in every word that Uncle Seth had told them about the Western state of Oregon, about its endless acres of beautiful, fertile land waiting to be claimed and cultivated. Oregon needed families, said Uncle Seth; honest, God-fearing families who were not afraid of a hard journey and hard work when they got there.

When Uncle Seth talked about Oregon his eyes shone and his whole face lit up. Ruth loved Uncle Seth, so much like her own father to look at, but with something extra and different about him, and she thought that Oregon must be a wonderful land to make him look like that.

Uncle Seth's blue eyes were twinkling now, above his large, sunburnt nose and black whiskers, as he looked about the table. "I thought you'd all be pleased," he said. "It'll be a busy day for us tomorow, goodbye to our friends on Sunday, then first thing Monday morning we'll be off."

Ruth's hearty appetite failed her, and for once she could not finish her meal. She wanted to get up and dance around the room for joy. But she clasped her hands tightly together in her lap and waited until everyone else had finished.

When the meal was over Uncle Seth and John and David pushed back their chairs, put on their caps and went out to do the evening chores. Ruth wished she might join them right away, but of course she could not. There were the dishes to do, and the twins to be washed and undressed and put to bed. She hurried so fast that a plate slipped through her fingers and broke on the stone floor.

"Oh, Ruth!" said Mary Rebecca in exasperation. "Not another plate!" But Aunt Susanna was not cross. "I guess Ruthie's excited," she said kindly, "'Becca and I will see to the little ones tonight, Ruth. You have a run outside. I guess you won't settle until you do."

Ruth threw her a grateful look, grabbed her bonnet and ran to the door. The evening was a typical late-April one, mild and dewy-soft. She capered across to the barn lot, where Uncle Seth and John were feeding and bedding down the wagon horses, and peeped in at

them for a moment. Sam, the sheepdog, was lying near the doorway waiting for them, and she patted his grizzled head before running on to the cow-stalls.

David was there milking Polly, the little tan-coloured heifer, the only cow they had left. Polly had a little calf who had been sold to the new owners, but Polly herself would be travelling with them on the journey. Ruth pulled up an extra stool and sat down beside David, stroking Polly's velvety flank.

"Want a go?" grinned David, but Ruth shook her head. She was learning to milk and could do it quite well, already better than Mary Rebecca, who shrank back if Polly so much as twitched her tail. But this evening she felt too excited to sit still for long. She watched the creamy milk froth and hiss into the pail for a moment, then got up and wandered out again. She was glad that Polly and Sam and the horses would be going on the journey with them.

The sun was going down like a big red ball in a streaky orange and red sky. Ruth stood and looked at it, remembering the rhyme which said that a red sky at night was the shepherd's delight. It would be a fine day tomorrow. She wondered whether there were red skies in Oregon, and how long it would be before she stood watching the sun go down there.

CHAPTER THREE

GETTING READY

Ruth thought that she would not be able to sleep one wink for excitement. But one moment she was climbing into bed beside Mary Rebecca, and the next, it seemed, she was opening her eyes to see the early light filtering in through the bedroom window. Mary Rebecca was already out of bed and dressed and was neatly braiding her long, smooth, corn-coloured hair. Ruth yawned and lay watching her sleepily for a moment, not wanting to leave the comfort of the warm bed. But her cousin had heard the yawn and turned her head from the little looking glass on the dressing-chest.

"Ruth," she called softly. "Are you awake? It's half-past five. We must get up early today."

All at once Ruth remembered that this was the day for getting ready, and she was wide awake in a flash. She flung back the blankets and bounced out of bed, almost knocking over the water-jug in her haste. She washed quickly in the cold water, and scrambled out of her flannel nightgown and into her long underwear and petticoats, her blue calico dress and everyday apron. Mary Rebecca turned back the bedclothes to air the bed, then picked up the hairbrush again to brush and braid her cousin's hair.

"Tck, tck," she clicked, dragging the brush through the tangles in Ruth's unruly copper curls. "What a mop! Anyone would think you had been dragged backwards through a haystack!"

Every morning Mary Rebecca said almost the same

thing, but it was no use Ruth telling her that she could not help the crinkly way her hair grew. She sat meekly until her cousin had finished, then they made the bed and went downstairs together.

Aunt Susanna had the twins already washed and dressed, and they were sitting in their high chairs feeding themselves with oatmeal in the usual messy way of small children.

"Ugh!" said Mary Rebecca. "Your hair is full of oatmeal, Daniel. Give me the spoon and let me help."

She began to spoon food into the eager mouth of her small brother with the air of a mother bird, and Ruth did the same for his twin. Then they gave each child a mug of milk and went to help Aunt Susanna with the other morning work. As well as getting breakfast there was the morning's milk to strain into bowls and set aside for the cream to rise, there was last night's milk to be skimmed, and there were preparations for the big baking and churning Aunt Susanna planned to do before the journey. By the time the men came in, Ruth's stomach was gnawing with hunger.

"My stomach feels as though my throat's been cut," she said cheerfully as Aunt Susanna passed plates of fried bacon and crisp fried bread. Immediately she felt an air of disapproval descend on the room.

"Ruth Carey!" said Mary Rebecca, shocked. "What a dreadful thing to say."

"Pa used to say it, sometimes," said Ruth defensively.

"Well, it's not a very nice expression," said Aunt Susanna gently but firmly, with her eye on David and the twins. "Please remember not to use it again, Ruth."

Ruth gulped and nodded her head. It was still so hard sometimes to remember what was the right thing to say and do, and what was not. It seemed that sometimes she just opened her mouth and bad words came out by themselves.

But Uncle Seth was saying, "She'll remember, won't you, Scatterbrain?" and his eyes were twinkling so she knew he wasn't really cross. She cheered up, ate her breakfast and listened eagerly as plans for the day were discussed. Uncle Seth and John had already got the wagon bows and the canvas cover or 'tilt' on the big wagon. Now everything must be loaded into it: farm implements, and household goods, sacks of grain, food for themselves and the animals—everything except the bedding and table and chairs and odds and ends which would be left till the last morning. The stalls and pens must be cleaned ready for the new owners, and everything prepared for a long, long journey.

Ruth wished that she might help the men, but of course she couldn't. There was far, far too much to be done in the farmhouse. Immediately after breakfast Aunt Susanna set her to churn, while she and Mary Rebecca washed all the dirty clothes which had been soaking in tubs in the wash-house all night. The family must start their journey clean.

Ruth turned and turned the handle of the wooden churn, hearing the cream splash and slosh inside. She used first one arm and then the other, changing sides as each in turn grew tired. It seemed a long time until the butter 'came', but it did at last, leaving the little window in the churn clear except for blobs of yellow butter.

"Now," said Aunt Susanna, "you help Mary Rebecca peg out the clothes while I wash this and salt it. It will be one more crock of butter to use on the journey."

Afterwards they all helped to bake. The big kitchen grew warm and steamy and full of delicious smells as bread and cakes and pies were cooked and set to cool on the table. At noon, dinner was eaten in a hurry. Aunt Susanna did not even sit down; she just took a bite now and then as she bustled back and forth between stove and table and back again.

Ruth felt she had done a good morning's work. Perhaps this afternoon Aunt Susanna would let her go outdoors and see what exciting things John and David and Uncle Seth had been doing. But not a bit of it.

"The house must have a good cleaning," said Aunt Susanna briskly as they finished the dishes. "We'll start with the bedrooms."

And they began giving the farmhouse the most thorough 'going-over' it had ever known. Carpets and rugs had already been rolled up and most of them sold or given away, blinds had been taken down, ornaments and small objects carefully packed. Now from attic to cellar they scoured and scrubbed and polished until the bare rooms shone and Ruth's very bones ached with weariness. She could not understand why all this cleaning had to be done just when they were going away, and said so. "The house doesn't really need so much cleaning—why can't we just leave it as it is?" she asked.

This was enough to make Aunt Susanna throw up her hands in horror. "What—leave a dirty house for the next people to move into!" she exclaimed. "I declare my conscience would never give me a minute's peace if I did such a thing."

So the scouring and the scrubbing went on. And after supper they all had to have baths, as it was Saturday night. Ruth had scarcely been out of doors all day, but she was too tired to care. Her feet dragged as she and Mary Rebecca took their candles and went upstairs to their bedroom. Mary Rebecca was pale and there were dark circles of fatigue under her eyes.

"What a day," sighed Ruth, setting down the candle and beginning to unhook her dress. "I've never, never been so tired."

"You've worked hard all day," said Mary Rebecca. "Mother and I wouldn't have been able to manage without you."

Ruth felt a warm glow. It wasn't often that she had words of praise from her older cousin. She knelt quickly and said her prayers, then leaned over and gave Mary Rebecca a kiss as they climbed into bed. How good it was to sink into its feather-filled softness and stretch out her aching limbs!

"Thank goodness it's Sunday tomorrow," said Mary Rebecca, and she blew out the candle.

CHAPTER FOUR

THE LAST SUNDAY AT HOME

Aunt Susanna let the girls sleep late next day and it was almost seven o'clock when they awoke. When they got downstairs the morning work was done, breakfast was ready, and they had nothing to do but sit down and eat it! How bare and clean the kitchen looked.

"Are we going to church the same as usual?" asked Ruth.

"Of course," said Uncle Seth, a little surprised. "Why should we not?"

Ruth didn't know, but when she thought about it, it did seem that a Sunday without church would be unthinkable in her uncle's household. She wondered how they would manage when they were on the trail. There would be no churches on the prairies and plains.

She asked Cousin John about it as she helped him to hitch the chestnut team, Belle and Benny, to the light wagon for the drive into town. John pushed back his cap and scratched his dark, curly head.

"Why, I guess we'll have a service in the open air," he said. "It's people that make up a church, after all, not a building. And I guess God doesn't mind where we are when we worship Him."

Ruth had often wondered about God, and she wondered about Him now as they were getting ready for church and as they drove into town behind the sleek backs of Belle and Benny. She sometimes imagined Him as someone kind and benevolent, a nice old man with a long white beard, and sometimes as a fierce, stern person dealing out punishment to sinners. She could not understand how it was that Uncle Seth and Aunt Susanna and John talked about and prayed to God as though He were someone they knew personally; 'as if He was their friend,' she thought, and realised that she had spoken the words aloud. But they were all climbing out of the wagon and no-one had noticed.

She went on wondering as they went quietly into the little building and sat in a row in the seats. Uncle Seth and Aunt Susanna each held one of the twins, and the little ones were quiet and good as though they sensed that they must be on their best behaviour.

The preacher announced the first hymn and they all got up and sang. Ruth glanced sideways at Mary Rebecca, who had the best voice of all the family, and who looked so pure and good in her sprigged muslin dress with her corn-coloured hair smooth and shining under her best bonnet.

"Oh, how I love Jesus, because He first loved me," sang Mary Rebecca, looking demurely down at her hymnbook, her voice ringing out silvery and sweet.

But was it all true? thought Ruth. She was sure that Jesus loved Mary Rebecca, who was so good, but she doubted whether He loved her, Ruth Elizabeth Carey. She was altogether too bad and troublesome to be loved by Jesus, the Son of God. She decided that she would ask Uncle Seth about it, when she had a chance.

During the service the preacher made a little speech of farewell to the Careys and the other farming families who were leaving home to pioneer to the West. Then he prayed for them and asked God to go with them, protect them on their long journey and bless them in the new land. Everyone said, Amen.

All the pioneer families from the church had been asked to a farewell dinner at the preacher's house next door to the church. There were more than thirty men, women and children and they couldn't possibly all squeeze into the house, so long tables had been set up in the garden. The ladies from the chuch were bustling to and fro with steaming plates and dishes, and mouth-watering smells came from the kitchen.

David and Ruth approached the table, sniffing hungrily.

"I smell turkey—and chicken pie—and onion gravy," David said in a whisper, because they mustn't talk loudly in company.

"I smell roast potatoes, and roast beef, and pumpkin pie," said Ruth.

There was all that and more. Everyone ate and ate, until even Ruth and David were so full they could hardly move. It was nearly as good as a Christmas or Thanksgiving dinner! All through the meal a buzz of conversation went on among the grown-ups. They were discussing lots of things, but mainly the big trip West. Ruth listened, wishing she could join in and ask questions about things she didn't understand, but of course she couldn't do that.

Towards the end of the meal yesterday's hard work began to catch up with her, and the buzz of talk seemed to grow fainter. Her eyelids drooped, and before long it seemed that she was no longer at the preacher's house, or at the farm, but back with her father in the little shack they had last lived in. She was sitting by herself waiting for him to come home, hoping that he was sober and would bring some food. But she didn't really need food, because her stomach was already full. Then something sharp was digging her in the ribs, and she woke with a start.

"You fell asleep," hissed David in her ear. "Look, everyone's finished."

The table was almost deserted, the men had gone off to sit and talk in little groups, and the ladies were clearing up. Fortunately Aunt Susanna and Mary Rebecca were among the helpers and had not noticed her lapse. It was considered very rude to fall asleep in company.

The smaller children, including the twins, had been laid down on beds to rest, and the bigger ones were standing about in little groups in the preacher's garden. They were not allowed to play games on a Sunday, so all they did was talk. Ruth straightened her dress and smoothed her hair and she and David went over to the nearest group of boys. They were sitting on the grass and of course they were talking about the trip. Ruth sat on the grass and listened. One of the big boys, Robert Snow, was boasting about how well he could shoot. "I tell you, you needn't be afraid of wolves while I'm around," he was saying. "Any wolf that comes within a hundred yards of me is as good as dead."

"What about Indians, Bob?" asked someone else, and the big boy laughed.

"Indians, too," he said. "Wolves and Indians are only good for one thing—target practice."

Some of the boys laughed, but Ruth did not like the way the big boy talked.

"But Indians are not like wolves," she said. "Wolves are wild animals, and Indians are people, like us."

Robert Snow turned and looked at her with a sneer.

"Indians are savages," he said. "Not in the least like us. And who asked your opinion, Miss Carrot-hair Carey?"

Ruth's cheeks grew red and she felt angry. She was not a bit afraid of a big bully like Robert Snow, and was about to reply when Mary Rebecca's voice could be heard calling, "Ruth! Ruth! Where are you?"

Ruth scrambled to her feet and hurried off towards the house.

"You have been sitting on the ground," scolded Mary Rebecca, brushing bits of grass off her cousin's skirt.

"I'm sorry," said Ruth meekly. She was glad she hadn't been seen talking to boys, which in Mary Rebecca's opinion was a far worse thing to do. But for the rest of the afternoon she had to sit sedately indoors on a sofa and listen to the conversation of her elders.

There was another service in the evening, but at last it was over, everyone had shaken hands with them and wished them well, and they were on their way home in the wagon. Ruth helped John to unhitch Belle and Benny, rub them down and give them a feed of oats. She loved the horses and was glad that these two would be going with them on the journey.

After supper, when the twins were in bed, they all sat round for the last time in the bare parlour and Uncle Seth read to them from the big Bible, as he always did on Sundays. This evening he read part of the story of the children of Israel who had left Egypt and journeyed across the desert until they reached the Promised Land. Ruth thought that this sounded a little like the pioneering families going to Oregon, but of course it wasn't really the same. They were leaving comfortable homes behind them, while Moses had led his people out of slavery. Uncle Seth must have read her thoughts, because he said, "We are like the children of Israel in one important way—God led them to the Promised Land, and I believe with all my heart that He is leading us to Oregon. I should not be going if I did not believe this. Long ago, soon after I first trusted the Lord Jesus as my Saviour, I learned that

He must be my Lord, too. I must do with my life as He wants, and He has told me that He wants me in Oregon, to live and serve Him there. So none of you must be afraid of our long journey—if we are obeying the Lord all that happens must be according to His will."

He closed the Bible, and stood up and bowed his head and prayed. Ruth felt comforted and cheered by her uncle's words, but she was still a little puzzled. Uncle Seth really did talk to God like the men in the Bible had done. It came to her suddenly that this was how he was different from her own father, though they had been brothers—it was Uncle Seth's faith in God that made him so fine and good. She wanted to ask more, but her head was drooping and her eyelids beginning to close again. The clock struck nine, and, for the very last time at the farmhouse in the East, it was bedtime.

CHAPTER FIVE

BEGINNING THE JOURNEY

What a hustle and a bustle there was in the morning! Everyone was up before it was light, breakfast was eaten in a hurry, and last minute preparations were made. Ruth and Mary Rebecca flew around under the direction of Aunt Susanna, fetching, carrying, running to the yard with armfuls of bedding to stow away in the wagon, and back again to the now almost empty house. The men and David were busily employed in the barns and stable, making sure that everything was left in apple-pie order.

By seven o'clock everything was ready. The horses stood hitched to the wagon, impatient to begin. They were sleek and plump, and their smooth chestnut sides shone with health and good spirits. Long journeys didn't worry them! Polly the cow stood beside the wagon, cropping at the fresh spring grass. She would follow tied behind the wagon to begin with. Then when they joined the big caravan she would be herded together with all the other cattle. Sam lay beside the wagon, eyes shining and ears pricked eagerly, sensing that adventure lay ahead. He did not mind leaving his old home as long as he could be with his own dear family. He was ready to travel with them and help protect them from all danger.

Aunt Susanna and the children tied on their sunbonnets for the last time in their old home. Mary Rebecca and her mother had both cried a little as they looked round the bare, clean rooms which had been their home for so long and where such happy times had been spent. Ruth's heart ached for her aunt and cousin. She felt like crying too, but she had been here only a year and they had lived here for many years, so of course it must be much worse for them. She took a hand of each of them and squeezed comfortingly.

"Oh dear," sniffed Aunt Susanna, "I do hope we're doing the right thing."

"Of course we are," said Ruth stoutly.

Just then Uncle Seth appeared in the doorway, strong and reassuring. "All ready?" he asked and picked up a twin in each arm from where they had been sitting on the scrubbed floor.

"Yes—we're all ready," said Aunt Susanna, with a straightening of her shoulders. She dabbed her eyes with her handkerchief and managed to smile at her husband. "All ready," she repeated.

None of them looked back as they closed the door for the last time and walked to where the wagon waited. David was already aboard, grinning from under the canvas tilt, impatient to be off. Uncle Seth put down the twins, helped his wife aboard and handed the two little ones up to her. Then he helped up Mary Rebecca. But Ruth had already scrambled up over the wagon wheel and had joined David inside the wagon. They all settled themselves as comfortably as they could on boxes placed specially for the purpose.

Uncle Seth and John swung themselves up on to the front seat, chirruped to the horses, and they were off, bumping steadily along down the hill away from the farm. At the bend in the road Ruth peeped round the tilt for one last glimpse of the farm. There it was, a huddle of grey buildings at the top of the rise, lonely in the morning light. She watched until it went out of sight behind the trees. A large lump had come up in her throat, but she swallowed it down firmly and thought, 'The wagon is our home now.'

A kind of pen had been made for the twins among the carefully loaded goods in the wagon. A small clear space had been surrounded with sacks of grain and cornmeal, covered with blankets and padded with a pillow or two. This made a nice, safe, comfortable place for them to play, and when they grew tired they could curl up and go to sleep on the blankets. A box with the little ones' toys and building-blocks had been put there too, and in the trustful way of little children Debbie and Daniel were soon playing happily in their own special place. Aunt Susanna sat near them on the left side, with Mary Rebecca and Ruth opposite. David was between his father and John in front, feeling very important and hoping that he would be allowed to hold the reins by himself sometimes. Sam trotted beside the wagon, his plumy tail flying like a flag.

The day was a fine one, soft and balmy, with a pleasant little breeze. Whenever they passed a homestead or someone riding or working in their fields, the person would wave and call to them, wishing them well. They trundled past the little white school-house, with Miss Thatcher's house next door. It was too early yet for school, but Ruth's sharp eyes caught a movement in one of the windows.

"There's Miss Thatcher—she's waving to us," said David from his perch in front. Sure enough, it was Miss Thatcher at the window, with a white handkerchief fluttering in her hand. Ruth jumped up and waved back and shouted, "Goodbye, goodbye, Miss Thatcher." Then she noticed Mary Rebecca frowning. "I thought shouting wouldn't matter in the wagon," she said in a small voice.

"Wherever we are, we must not forget to behave

like ladies," said Mary Rebecca. She would not permit herself more than a polite wave and a prim farewell bow to her teacher.

"Yes, Mary Rebecca," said Ruth, and she sat down again.

Soon they were nearing the neighbour's homestead where they were to meet the rest of the party. Sure enough, three loaded wagons, each with its respective family, cattle and horses, were waiting there. The Carey wagon drew to a halt and the men got down to talk with the others while they waited for the two remaining wagons. Ruth wished she could get down too and run to talk to the other children, but Aunt Susanna told her to sit still.

"You'll wear yourself out, climbing in and out," she said.

The other wagons soon came rumbling along, one with the Robertson family and one with the Snows. Ruth saw Robert Snow sitting beside his father. She did not like him very much, but she suddenly remembered what he had said about wolves and Indians.

"Will there be wolves where we camp tonight?" she asked Aunt Susanna.

"Good gracious no, child!" said her aunt emphatically. "We won't have travelled many miles by tonight. We won't see anything of wolves until we reach the prairies—and not then, I hope. So don't trouble your head."

Ruth did not like to say that she was not troubled by the thought of wolves. In fact, it was exciting to think of them surrounding the camp with themselves snug and safe inside the wagon. She peeped round the tilt again as Uncle Seth climbed into the front seat and they set off again. What a lot of dust was kicked up when all the wagons rolled along together! People shouted from one to the other, cows lowed and dogs barked. It was very exciting. She darted from one side to the other, trying to see all she could, until Aunt Susanna said in exasperation. "Sit still, Ruth, do! I declare it makes me feel tired to have you keep jumping about like that."

So Ruth went back to Mary Rebecca and sat down beside her and kept still for a long time.

CHAPTER SIX

MAKING CAMP

By nightfall it seemed to Ruth that they must have travelled a very long way. They had gone up hill and down dale, through woods, over little streams and past strange homesteads and farmlands. The country was now quite unfamiliar. Even when Ruth's father was alive and they had moved around a lot as he tried different jobs, they had never spent a whole long day travelling like this.

They stopped for the night at last near a clear little creek which would provide good drinking water for themselves and the animals. The men drove the wagons to the grassy bank, unhitched the horses and watered them before tethering them to graze. Everyone climbed down stiffly from the wagons, glad to stretch their limbs after sitting still for so long.

Ruth ran up to John, who was giving the horses a rub down before taking them to drink at the creek.

"How many miles have we come?" she asked eagerly.

"About nineteen or twenty, I guess," he said, giving Benny an encouraging slap on the neck. "Not bad going for the first day."

Twenty miles seemed a very long way indeed.

"We'll soon get to Oregon," said Ruth, and John laughed and gave her braid a tweak as he led the horses away.

Ruth ran back to the wagon, where Aunt Susanna was organising the rest of the family, glad to be able to bustle around again instead of sitting still all the time.

"Ruth—David, you two collect some wood for a fire," she called from the wagon where she was sorting out her pots and pans from the mounds of supplies. Mary Rebecca lifted down the twins, who stood side by side at first, blinking and looking a little bewildered. But they soon recovered and began to play and run about on the grass, glad of the freedom after their long day in the wagon.

"There should be wood along the creek bank," said David, grabbing Ruth's hand. They ran to the stream, where some of the other children were also gathering wood and fetching water. Ruth would have liked to linger and talk, to explore and paddle in the stream and look for fish, but there was no time for that. Everyone had a job to do and must get on with it. The camp was soon a hive of activity. Fires were being lit and suppers cooked, there were sounds of babies crying and people calling to each other. The cattle and horses drank thirstily at the stream or grazed on the lush green grass which grew along the banks.

When Ruth and David got back to the wagon with their armfuls of dry brushwood, Uncle Seth had already kindled a crackling fire of dry twigs. He had driven two forked sticks into the ground with another strong one across them to support the kettle, and the small supply of water from the wagon was already boiling for coffee. Aunt Susanna was busily mixing up some cornbread while Mary Rebecca sliced bacon into a pan. Uncle Seth had gone to milk Polly, and soon appeared with a foaming pail. John took another pail to the creek for water.

It was fun to eat supper in the open round the camp fire. Darkness was beginning to fall, but the circle of firelight, with the wood crackling cheerfully, seemed cosy and safe. Afterwards Uncle Seth read from the Bible and prayed, exactly as if they were at home. He thanked God for their safe day's journey and asked Him to watch over them during their first night on the trail.

The heads of the twins were already nodding sleepily, so as soon as prayers were finished Aunt Susanna and Mary Rebecca picked them up and prepared to put them to bed in the wagon.

"We'll need more water for the morning," said Aunt Susanna.

Ruth thought what fun it would be to run down to the stream in the mysterious twilight. She nudged David and said, "David and I will fetch some. Please may we?"

Aunt Susanna hesitated for a moment, but then she said, "Well, I suppose you may. But come straight back and don't forget which is our wagon."

"That's easy—ours is the one nearest the creek," said David.

They picked up the water pails and ran off before she decided to change her mind and make John go instead. A light dew was beginning to fall and the grass was slightly damp under their bare feet. The stream looked dark as they approached it, and it made friendly little chuckling sounds. There were willow trees growing thickly along the banks, which whispered in the evening breeze. From somewhere far away an owl hooted.

As they got to the creek they saw that someone else was there, also dipping up water into a pail. Another pail was on the bank beside him. He had his back to them, but he turned to put down his full pail as the children approached, and they recognised Robert

Snow. He was intent on his task and did not see Ruth and David.

"Let's give him a surprise," whispered David, and Ruth nodded gleefully. Treading carefully, they crept up behind the big boy as he bent to fill his second pail. As they reached him they jumped forward together, shouted "Boo!" and dropped their pails on the shingly creek bank, making a tremendous clatter. Robert Snow gave a great jump; he dropped his full pail, soaking his right trouser leg and boot, and was half-way up the bank towards the wagons before he realised what had alarmed him. When he saw Ruth and David grinning at him through the dusk he scowled and shook his fist at them.

"You young scoundrels—you should be horse-whipped," he said from between gritted teeth.

"Did you think we were Indians?" asked David innocently. But he was poised ready for flight. Like many of the smaller boys his ears had been boxed by the bully on more than one occasion. But the big boy only said, "You just wait, Carey," in a threatening voice as he retrieved his pails and strode away towards the wagons.

Ruth and David laughed so much that they had difficulty in filling their pails with water. They were still giggling as they climbed the bank and went towards the wagon, and the water kept slopping out of the pails. But they managed to get their faces straight before they walked into the circle of firelight. Aunt Susanna would not look very kindly on such a prank.

The camp was settling down for the night. Children were being tucked down inside the wagons, fires were dying out, and soon the grown-ups would be going to bed as well. Uncle Seth said it was 'early to bed, early to rise', even more so on the trail than it had been on the farm.

Some of the pioneers with large families had tents pitched beside the wagon to house the overflow. The Careys had a small tent, too, which John and David were to share. Ruth felt a little envious as she watched them put it up, and saw David wrap himself snugly in blankets for the night. She wished she was a boy—then she might be sleeping outdoors, too. But Aunt Susanna was calling, "Ruth—bedtime!" so she said goodnight to David and climbed into the wagon. It was very strange to be undressing in the dim interior, with only a layer of canvas between themselves and the starry sky. The twins were already fast asleep in a little nest between the two beds made up on the floor of the wagon, one for Aunt Susanna and Uncle Seth and the other for herself and Mary Rebecca. Even though they now lived in a wagon Aunt Susanna made them wash their faces, brush their hair and say their prayers before they got into bed. "We must not allow ourselves to become uncivilised," she said.

"I declare I won't sleep a wink," said Ruth as she lay down beside her cousin and gazed at the opening of the tilt, where a few bright stars showed in a patch of dark blue night sky.

"Yes, you will," said Mary Rebecca. "Just be quiet and lie still, and you'll be asleep before you know it."

And of course she was right. For a short while Ruth lay listening to the little snuffling sounds the twins made as they slept, and presently to a faint snoring from Mary Rebecca's side of the bed. Then her eyelids drooped, she gave a big sigh and remembered no more. The first day on the trail was over.

CHAPTER SEVEN

SUNDAY ON THE TRAIL

After a few days of travelling it seemed to Ruth that they had never known any other life, nor lived in any other home except the wagon. The days fell into a smooth routine: getting up early, seeing to breakfast and the chores, then breaking camp and setting off, travelling all day except for one stop at noon. Then it was stop again for the night, light fires, make camp, more chores, and go to bed in the wagon.

On the fourth day they crossed a river—not the little creeks which they often had to splash through, but a real, deep-flowing river. Two riders went through first to test the depth. John was now riding Beauty, a bay mare belonging to Farmer Robertson, and he was one of the two. Ruth's heart was in her mouth as the swift water splashed against Beauty's slender legs, rising quickly to stirrup level and covering John's feet. In mid-stream it almost reached the mare's shoulders and Ruth thought she would be forced to swim. But then the water-level was going down, and Beauty and John were scrambling, dripping but safe, up the opposite bank.

Then Uncle Seth and the other men drove their teams into the river with the wagons behind. Aunt Susanna had an arm firmly round each twin, and Ruth and Mary Rebecca held hands tightly as the water sloshed and splashed against the sides of the wagon. The horsemen were driving the cattle through the water, shouting and whipping them to keep them moving. For one dreadful moment, in mid-stream,

Ruth thought that everything, wagons, horses and cattle, would be swept together downstream in the rushing water. Then the danger was past and the horses were valiantly pulling them up the bank.

On Saturday they camped by another creek. When the chores were done and supper eaten, Uncle Seth went off to talk to the other men. Aunt Susanna heated more water over the fire, and they filled the bath-tub and took baths inside the wagon, dimly lit by the firelight from outside. Ruth was just climbing into bed, clean and scrubbed, when Uncle Seth came back. She heard him give a little grunt as he sat down beside the fire to talk to Aunt Susanna.

"Well, shall we be travelling tomorrow, Seth?" asked Aunt Susanna.

"No, tomorrow we rest," said Uncle Seth. "One or two of them wanted to press on, but most of us agreed that it would be better to rest over the Sabbath."

"The horses will be glad of the rest," said John, who was sitting whittling a stick, and Uncle Seth agreed. "We'll see if we can get a meeting together," he said. "Even without a real preacher I guess we can praise the Lord and keep His day holy."

So Ruth knew that Sunday, even on the trail, would be different from other days. When she woke next morning the sun was shining in, and her clean underwear and best dress was laid out for her to put on. As she dressed, Ruth thought how quickly things could change in just a week. Last Sunday they had been at home on the farm, now they had travelled many miles and were on their way to the West.

The meeting was held on the creek bank, with the sun sparkling on the water, and nesting birds chirping in the willows. The sky was a soft blue, with fluffy little clouds floating across it, and the ground was clothed with tender new spring green. The men brought out the wagon seats and arranged them for the ladies and themselves to sit on, but the children could sit on fallen branches or on the ground if they were careful of their clothes. Ruth thought that this was a great improvement on ordinary church and said so in a whisper to David as the meeting began. Then she caught Mary Rebecca's stern eye upon her and lapsed into silence.

One of the men had a concertina, which he played to accompany the hymns. Mr Robertson prayed, Mr Danvers read from the Bible, and Uncle Seth said a few words instead of a sermon. Ruth thought that Uncle Seth was easier to understand than any preacher she had heard, but there were still things about the Bible which puzzled her. Why did Jesus have to die on a cruel cross when He was the best and kindest man who had ever lived? Did God really love everyone in the world, naughty people like herself as well as good ones like Mary Rebecca? And how did loving God make one different from people who did not? There were so many things she did not understand. But having a meeting in the open air was much better than going to church. When Ruth looked at the clear blue sky and breathed in the soft spring air, even she could believe that God was not far away.

Ruth was quieter than usual as she helped her aunt and cousin to prepare dinner. Going to church always made her thoughtful, even when the church was a creek bank.

After dinner Aunt Susanna put the twins down to sleep, and she and Mary Rebecca sat down to read just inside the wagon. John went to talk with some of the big boys sitting by the creek, and David tagged after him. Ruth wished that she could go too, but of course it would never be allowed. She yawned and resigned herself to an afternoon of sitting still and doing nothing.

Then Uncle Seth poked his head inside the wagon and said, "Would anyone like to come for a walk?"

Ruth jumped up at once and said, "Oh, yes." Then she remembered to go and ask Aunt Susanna nicely if she might go, and was thankful when permission was given.

"But remember your sunbonnet," Aunt Susanna added. "This sun will ruin your complexion."

Ruth did not worry much about her complexion, but obediently she put on her sunbonnet. Uncle Seth swung her down from the wagon, took her hand in his big, work-roughened one, and together they walked upstream beside the sparkling water.

It was nice to walk and talk alone with Uncle Seth. He was so much like her father had been, and yet so different in some ways. He answered all Ruth's questions so patiently and knew so much about all kinds of things. The sun shone warmly on them as they walked.

"We'll need this kind of weather this time next year," said Uncle Seth.

'Shall we be in Oregon then?" asked Ruth, and he nodded. "God willing, we'll be there next fall, before the snow and the storms come," he said. "We'll build a little house for the winter, and then in spring we'll begin ploughing and sowing our first crops." His eyes shone as they always did when he talked of Oregon.

"What will we live on all the winter?" wondered Ruth. She knew that the stores they had with them would not last a whole year.

"Why, we'll live off the land," said Uncle Seth.

"Oregon will be full of game, I guess—deer and rabbit and bear and wild fowl, and fish in the creeks. We'll be able to shoot all the meat we need, and trade the furs for other things. And we have Polly for milk and butter and cheese. We should be able to last out the winter in comfort, God willing."

"Why do you always say, God willing?" asked Ruth curiously.

"Because we want to do what *He* wants," said Uncle Seth.

They had walked a long way upstream. When Ruth looked back she could see the wagons, a little cluster of white canvas covers at the bend of the creek. Uncle Seth sat down on a fallen branch of willow and took Ruth on his knee. She liked to sit on Uncle Seth's knee and smell the nice scent of wood-smoke and horses and clean, starched linen which lingered about him on Sundays. Ruth remembered all the things she had meant to ask about God, and she said, "Uncle Seth, how do you know that God loves us all?"

"Because He tells us that He does in His word, which is the Bible," said Uncle Seth. He went on to tell Ruth how God made the first man, who was called Adam, and gave him a beautiful garden to live in with his wife, Eve. Adam and Eve had everything they could possibly need; they had fresh air and sunshine and animals and birds and flowers, plenty of food and pleasant work to do, and they should have been very happy.

Ruth nodded her head in agreement. "With all those things, anyone would be happy," she said.

But Uncle Seth went on to tell of how Satan had come and tempted Adam and Eve, and how they had done the one thing God had told them they must not, and so had become sinners. "And every single person born since then," said Uncle Seth, "is a sinner, too. And no sinner can go to be with God when he or she dies."

Ruth nodded again. She knew that there were many wicked people in the world, and that wicked people could not go to heaven, but only to a dreadful place called hell. She knew that she was a sinner, because of all the naughty things she did and said and thought.

"But you are not a sinner, Uncle Seth," she said.

"Oh, but I am, Ruthie," corrected her uncle. "That is, I was born a sinner, but the day came when I realised that God made a way for me to be forgiven by sending His only Son, Jesus, to die in my place. I only had to confess my sin, and receive Him into my heart and I would be forgiven. And so I did, and I am. And that's how I know God loves me."

"And did it really work, Uncle Seth?" asked Ruth, feeling her eyes grow round as she looked at her uncle.

"It did, Ruthie, it did indeed," he said, hugging her close in the circle of his arm. "I guess I've been a hundred times happier since then than ever I was before. I know my sins are forgiven and that I've a place waiting for me in heaven. And by praying and reading God's word I get to know what He wants me to do day by day."

So that was why Jesus died—because He loved people so much; and that was why Uncle Seth seemed so happy and fine and good. It was because he trusted God and tried to obey Him in every way.

"And have Aunt Susanna and John and Mary Rebecca all trusted Jesus, too?" asked Ruth.

"I am thankful to say they have," said Uncle Seth. "I guess David and the twins are a mite young yet, although no-one is too young to come to Jesus as soon as they understand. We pray for them, and for you, too."

"Do you?" asked Ruth, her eyes wide again.

He nodded. "How about it, Ruthie? Don't you think you'd like your sins forgiven too?"

At first Ruth thought she would. It would be nice to be like Uncle Seth and Aunt Susanna and John. Then a perverse little voice seemed to say in her mind, "But then you wouldn't be able to have fun—you'd have to be so good all the time—you'd have to be just like Mary Rebecca?" She didn't stop to think that Mary Rebecca was Mary Rebecca, that Ruth was Ruth, that everyone was different and that God intended this to be so. She listened to the little voice and said, "I—I don't know, Uncle Seth. Please can we go back to the wagon now. I'm tired."

Uncle Seth did not press her. He set her on her feet and stood up himself, carefully brushing them both down. Then he took her hand and they walked downstream towards the camp.

But as they neared the wagons Uncle Seth said, "You just think it over, Ruth. And remember that we'll all be praying for you."

CHAPTER EIGHT

COYOTES AND WOLVES

By the time another two weeks had passed they had reached the small town where they were to join the big wagon train. They camped there for a few days, to give any latecomers a chance to join them, and to make sure that all was ready for a long trip. Aunt Susanna said that this was the last real town they would see for a long time, because soon they would be on the open prairies where there were no towns. So anything that needed to be bought from a store must be bought now.

Aunt Susanna was glad of the rest from travelling because now she could catch up with the work. Uncle Seth fixed up a washing line for her, they boiled kettles and pans of water and she and Mary Rebecca washed all the dirty clothes. Ruth helped by pegging them out while her aunt and cousin aired all the bedding and swept and tidied inside the wagon. Debbie and Daniel romped and frolicked like puppies around her feet, excited by the activity of the camp.

"Horses, horses," laughed Daniel, pointing a chubby finger.

"Horses," echoed Debbie, clinging to Ruth's apron.

When the clothes were all flapping on the line Ruth took the twins by the hands and led them round the camp for a little walk. She had never seen so many covered wagons, all with a full load of men, women and children and their goods and chattels. Horses, cattle and dogs milled around, some tethered and some herded by small boys, and there was a continuous noise of lowing, barking and shouting. Everything seemed strange and unfamiliar, and suddenly Ruth was nervous of so many strange sights and sounds. She held the twins' hands firmly and hurried them back to the security of their own wagon.

Two days later the wagons left the little town and set out West again. The wagons travelled in long columns, with men on horses riding ahead to act as scouts. The cattle were herded by more men and boys on horseback. Ruth would have loved to scout or herd cattle, but all the women and girls had to ride in the wagons.

When they made camp the wagons were now driven together in a big circle and fastened together with the shafts and chains. All the cooking and work was done inside this circle. The cattle and horses were tethered at night, and there were always men who took it in turns to keep watch and guard the camp. Ruth knew without being told that they were leaving civilised farming country behind and would soon be in open prairie lands where there were many dangers.

Every Sunday was a day of rest. Some of the pioneers would have travelled seven days a week and treated Sunday just like any other day. But there were many, like Uncle Seth, who wished to keep it as God's holy day, and they had succeeded in doing so. There was even a real preacher travelling with the wagons, so now regular services could be held.

One day Ruth realised that the countryside had changed. They had travelled many miles that day, and had not seen a cultivated field or a wood or even a house for a long time. Now all around them was nothing but tall, rustling buffalo-grass as far as the eye could see, and the blue sky stretching up from the horizon. They had reached the prairies.

A creek ran through the open land in a little gully,

and they camped beside it for the night. As cramped limbs were stretched and chores begun, John came up to the wagon and reached inside it for his gun and powder-horn.

"Time to shoot some supper before it gets dark," he said cheerfully.

For some time now the men had been shooting game to help out supplies. Rabbits, prairie chickens and sometimes even deer were roasted over the camp fires and enjoyed by everyone.

It was not long before John came home with a small antelope over the front of his saddle. He and Uncle Seth quickly skinned and dressed it, Aunt Susanna cooked some and gave some to her nearest neighbours, and at supper they all sat around enjoying the sizzling steaks with freshly-baked cornbread. Sam had his share, and after the meal Aunt Susanna hung up the rest of the meat outside the wagon to be used next day.

Ruth was awakened suddenly in the night by a sound from outside. She lay still, listening for a moment. Now nothing could be heard except the soft breathing of the other occupants of the wagon, the grass rustling in the night wind, and the occasional snort and snuffle from the horses tethered outside. Perhaps she had imagined that strange sound. She was drifting off to sleep when suddenly it came again, a faint, eerie howling sound, a little like a dog but wilder and somehow frightening. It came again, still far away but a little nearer now. Ruth heard Sam growl softly under the wagon and knew that he heard it too.

Then suddenly there were different sounds very near indeed—whinings and whimperings accompanied by scufflings and pattering feet. Something was right there outside the wagon.

Sam snarled again and launched himself to the attack. At the very same moment Ruth sat up in bed and screamed, "Uncle Seth! Uncle Seth! There are wolves after us!"

Immediately all was confusion. Uncle Seth seized his gun, sprang out of bed and leapt from the wagon. The boys could be heard scrambling from the tent, and everyone else woke up. The twins began to cry, and voices called as some of the men from the neighbouring wagons woke up and ran over to the Careys' wagon.

Ruth sat rigid with fear as Uncle Seth's gun cracked out. There was a snarling and a yapping, and a sound of something running away, then the sounds of men's voices talking and calling to their dogs. Aunt Susanna was soothing the twins, and as soon as they were quiet she came and sat beside Ruth, putting a comforting arm round her shaking shoulders. Mary Rebecca, who always slept deeply, had awakened at the sound of the shot and was sleepily asking what was the matter.

"It's all right," Aunt Susanna soothed them, "Nothing is going to hurt you."

Then Uncle Seth was climbing back into the wagon and hanging up his gun.

"What was it, Seth?" asked Aunt Susanna quickly.

"W—w—was it wolves?" gasped Ruth through chattering teeth.

"No—coyotes," said Uncle Seth. "It was all our fault, too, that they came so close to camp. They smelt the antelope we hung up outside and came to get themselves some supper. We should have known better than to leave it there, on the outside of the circle."

"And did they take the meat?" asked Aunt Susanna.

"They did," said Uncle Seth. "And serve us right for not knowing better. We're nothing better than tenderfeet," he added with a disgusted grunt.

Ruth's trembling was growing less. Aunt Susanna gave her a last comforting pat and everyone lay down and tried to go back to sleep. Coyotes were far less frightening creatures than wolves. They would not attack people.

But as the camp became quiet again, the far-away eerie howling came to Ruth's ears once more, making her scalp prickle as though her hair was standing on end. She sat up again, careful not to disturb Mary Rebecca who had gone back to sleep.

"Uncle Seth," whispered Ruth through the darkness. "Are you asleep?"

"Not yet, Scatterbrain," came Uncle Seth's answering whisper. "What is it?"

"That howling—is it the coyotes?" asked Ruth. "It makes me shiver."

Uncle Seth listened for a moment before he replied. "No," he whispered at last. "Those are wolves howling. But don't be afraid—they're a long, long way across the prairie. And they wouldn't attack a big camp like ours. Now go to sleep."

Ruth felt comforted. Uncle Seth always spoke the truth. And even wolves could not hurt them if he was there to take care of them. But she couldn't help smiling wryly when she remembered how she had looked forward to hearing wolves howling round the camp. She hadn't imagined it would almost make her blood run cold with terror. She lay down and pulled the bedclothes over her head to shut out the sound of those eerie howling sounds floating across the prairie, and at last she fell asleep.

CHAPTER NINE

SURPRISE VISITORS

A few days later it was Sunday again and the travellers rested on the prairie. It was now nearly the end of May and the weather was getting hotter every day. All day long the sun beat down on them, and the only shade they had was the canvas cover of the wagon.

After the Sunday morning service, everyone was glad to rest. The women and girls sat in the wagons, which had both ends of the cover rolled open now so that a cooling breeze could blow through. The boys and men lounged and lay outside on the grass in whatever shade they could find. Some lay under the wagons, and they all talked about the trail and the journey, and how the weather had kept fine for them so far, and what they planned to do when they were settled in Oregon. Outside the circle of wagons the cattle and horses ranged free and grazed on the sweet prairie grass. They were glad of a day with no travelling, too.

In the Carey wagon the twins were restless. They had wakened early from their afternoon nap, and were tired of playing with the same toys. Soon Daniel had thrown a building block at Debbie, bruising her forehead and making her cry. She waited until his back was turned and then slyly crept up and sank her sharp little teeth into her twin's chubby leg. He roared loudly, as much with rage as with pain. Aunt Susanna and Mary Rebecca each hurriedly picked up a child and tried to soothe it.

"I declare I scarcely know what to do with them,"

said Aunt Susanna distractedly, rubbing the marks on Daniel's leg.

"They were never like this back home," agreed Mary Rebecca.

Ruth understood how the little ones felt. They were hot and weary and tired of being cooped up in the wagon. She often felt just the same way herself. "Shall I take them for a walk?" she offered.

Aunt Susanna gave her a grateful look. "That would be very kind of you, dear. Perhaps David will go with you. But don't go too far from the wagons, will you."

Ruth called to David, who was kicking his heels in the grass not far away, and they lifted the younger children to the ground and set off through the long grass away from the circle of wagons.

"Do you suppose the prairie goes on for ever?" asked Ruth, looking at the gently rolling landscape which stretched as far as the eye could see.

"Of course not," said David. "John says we'll be coming to mountains pretty soon. But I guess there'll be lots more prairies before we reach Oregon."

The twins were in their element. They toddled happily along, golden heads bobbing, laughing at the grasses which tickled their bare legs. They chattered together in their own special language, the best of friends again. This was much better than being shut up inside a stuffy wagon!

When they were a little distance away from the camp they sat down to rest in the grass. David and Ruth lay on their stomachs, chewing tough, sweet stalks of the tall grass, while the twins ran about picking bunches of prairie flowers and chasing the hundreds of little coloured butterflies which fluttered about. Sometimes a harmless little garter-snake slithered by near them, making ripples in the grass.

They talked for a little while, then lay silent. David rolled over on to his back and squinted at the blue sky, whistling tunelessly. Ruth cradled her head on her arms, feeling the warmth of the sun on her neck through her sunbonnet, and listening to the whistling, the soft chattering of the twins and the whispering of the grasses. Soon all these sounds seemed to merge into one soft humming sound, like a lullaby, and she felt her lids growing heavy and her eyes closing.

She came to with a start. David was tickling her cheek with a long grass and grinning at her.

"You were asleep," he said.

Ruth rolled over and sat up, rubbing her eyes. "Oh—was I?" Then she remembered the twins. "David—where are Debbie and Daniel?"

David looked about him vaguely. "Oh, they're somewhere about, I guess."

But when Ruth scrambled to her feet and looked around she could not see them anywhere. Her heart began to thump in alarm. "Debbie! Daniel!" she called anxiously. "Oh, David, why did you let me go to sleep! Help me to look for them."

They began to search through the long grass, calling all the while. How terrible if she had let the little ones wander off and get lost, Ruth thought miserably. And the poor little things would be most dreadfully frightened. Oh, how could she have gone to sleep like that!

It was with great relief that at last she heard a little voice answering their calls: "Ruth—Ruth, here we are." They had not wandered far at all, but were sitting side by side on the ground, their golden heads hidden in the tall grass. They were not at all frightened, indeed they looked very pleased with themselves as their brother and cousin came panting up.

"Nice—nice," said Debbie, and Ruth saw that both children were eating something. They had discovered a patch of bilberries, unripe because it was not yet June, and were busily picking them and cramming them into their mouths.

"Oh, Debbie—Daniel, you'll get a dreadful tummy-ache," said Ruth in dismay. She quickly pulled them to their feet, wiped their sticky little hands and faces on her apron and turned back towards the camp. Aunt Susanna would probably be cross, but at least no real harm had come to the little ones.

They were nearing the wagons when she heard David suddenly draw in his breath in a sharp gasp.

"What is it?" she asked, stopping in her tracks.

"Look," he said, pointing across the prairie to the West. Ruth looked. The sun was beginning to go down, a reddish ball in a streaky orange and yellow sky. Narrowing her eyes against its brightness Ruth could see that far away on the prairie something was moving. It looked like horses—horses with people on them, moving towards the camp. But there were no people here, except themselves and—her heart began to pound with fear and excitement. Could it be Indians?

"It's Injuns—I bet it is," said David excitedly. "Come on; we must warn the camp!"

They clasped the twins' hands tightly and flew into the camp, running up to the nearest group of settlers. The air of Sunday quiet was disturbed as everyone came crowding round to see what was the matter. The men looked solemn as they looked across the prairie and saw the group of horsemen approaching.

"It *is* Indians," said one sharp-eyed man. "I can see their feathers flying. Looks like they have some squaws and children with them, too."

A little ripple of alarm and uncertainty ran through the group. What could the Indians want? Were they peaceful or otherwise? Some of the men fingered their guns, but Uncle Seth said firmly, "Put away your fire-arms, Likely they'll be harmless enough unless we harm them first. And we won't. Anyway, there's no more than a dozen or so of them. And they wouldn't have women and children with them if they meant trouble."

Everyone could see the sense of this. But there was still an air of uneasiness as the little group of riders came nearer. Ruth could see feathers fluttering on the heads of some of them.

"I've got tummy-ache," whined Daniel suddenly. Ruth was still holding a twin by each hand. She had forgotten everything except those Indians coming nearer and nearer by the minute.

Aunt Susanna and Mary Rebecca had come out of the wagon, and Uncle Seth turned to them. "Susanna, take the children to the wagon. All womenfolk and children had better stay inside until we tell you other-wise."

Aunt Susanna gathered her flock together and hurried them into the wagon. Ruth was trembling but she just had to see what was happening outside. She went to the side of the wagon where there was a tiny rent in the canvas, and peeped through. All the women and children had disappeared inside their wagons. The men stood silently waiting. There was a soft thudding sound of horses' hooves on grass, and next moment the Indians, mounted on sturdy little ponies, were riding into the camp.

CHAPTER TEN

"GOD LOVES INDIANS"

Ruth stood and gazed in fascination. There were seven Indian men. They were tall and lean, with stern, hawk-nosed faces, and their skins were coppery-brown. Their hair was long and black and it was tied in a scalp-lock on the top of their heads and trimmed with waving, coloured feathers. The rest of their heads were shaved bare. They wore buckskin leggings trimmed with beads and fringes and feathers; tomahawks were in their belts and mocassins on their feet. All of them had guns resting lightly across the horses' shoulders.

The three Indian women were wrapped in brightly striped blankets, and their hair streamed black and heavy down their backs. One had a small saddlebag on her pony with a small child in it; another carried a bundle on her back in which the small black head of a baby could be seen. All of them rode sturdy little prairie ponies with no saddle or bridle, just a blanket to sit on.

Ruth forgot her fear as she gazed at them. The leading Indian stopped as they reached the wagons and said something that she could not understand. Then Uncle Seth stepped forward and spoke to them, and the Indian spoke again and waved his arms towards the wagons. Uncle Seth nodded and stepped back, and the Indians rode through the opening into the circle of wagons and dismounted. The settlers stood together in a bunch and watched them uneasily, but no one stirred.

"I think they just want to look around our camp,"

said Ruth excitedly from her spy-hole.

"Oh—I'm so frightened," said Mary Rebecca, and she began to sob. But Aunt Susanna was very calm. She carried on as though nothing was happening and told them not to be afraid. It made Ruth feel better just to watch her moving quietly about the wagon.

"I've got tummy-ache," said Daniel again, holding his plump little stomach.

Ruth remembered the green bilberries. She quickly told Aunt Susanna how she had let the twins wander off and pick the berries.

"Well—never mind," said Aunt Susanna. "I dare-say bed and a good dose of camomile tea will put them right. I'll give them some right away."

Ruth was relieved that her aunt was not cross. She turned back to the rent in the canvas. The Indians were walking about the camp, looking at the fires and the horses and cattle and dogs and peering into the tents and wagons. Their horses stood together in a bunch, waiting patiently.

Uncle Seth appeared in the doorway of the wagon. "I think they're Cheyennes. Susanna, if any of them want to come in here just be still and let them. Don't stop them touching anything or cross them in any way, and likely they'll soon go away."

Aunt Susanna nodded, and he went away. A moment later her face whitened as a black head and brown face appeared in his place, and one of the Indians came climbing into the wagon. It was the woman with the baby on her back.

Mary Rebecca shrank back and covered her face with her hands, and the twins began to whimper. Even David grew so pale that his freckles seemed to stand out. Ruth stood rigid against the canvas wall, watching as the woman poked about, looking curiously at all their belongings. She had a smooth, brown face, neither young nor old but somehow proud and fearless. A beaded leather band was around her head, and she wore a bright red and blue blanket and mocassins trimmed with more beads. The baby on her back was asleep, his little round black head just showing above the top of the bundle.

Aunt Susanna was marvellous. She carried on just as though the Indian woman was not there, and went on undressing the twins and putting them to bed. The woman finished prowling around the wagon and sat down on a box to watch her. The little baby woke up and stared inquisitively around with bright black eyes in its small brown face. It did not seem at all surprised to find itself in this strange place.

The children were all still and quiet. Aunt Susanna mixed a dose of camomile tea and gave it to each twin on a spoon. Debbie swallowed hers down, pulling a face, but Daniel would not. He yelled and threshed about, remembering how bitter the medicine had tasted last time. Aunt Susanna took hold of his nose with her free hand, he opened his mouth to protest indignantly, and next moment the spoon had popped in and the dose had gone down.

The very faintest flicker of a smile passed over the Cheyenne woman's face. She pointed to Daniel in the bed, then pointed to her mouth and rubbed her own stomach. Aunt Susanna nodded. She knew that the woman was asking if Daniel had stomach-ache. Perhaps she dosed her own little baby in the same way, thought Ruth.

The woman sat there for a long time, watching all that went on. Aunt Susanna picked up and folded the twins' clothes, then began to get things ready for supper, as if everything was just as usual. Ruth and

David and Mary Rebecca sat in a row, wide-eyed and wondering. The twins lost their fear of the strange lady and sat up to bounce and laugh on the bed. Their tummy-ache was better already and it was too soon yet for sleep.

At last the woman got up and went out of the wagon with her baby. Aunt Susanna sat down suddenly to rest, as if her legs had suddenly grown weak. Ruth got up and went back to her peep-hole. The Cheyennes were gathering together and getting on to their ponies again. They seemed to be satisfied with what they had seen about the camp. Without speaking a word they rode away from the wagons and across the prairie until they were just little black dots moving towards the setting sun, getting smaller and smaller.

Women and children poured from the wagons, dogs were released from restraining hands, and everyone talked together in relief and excitement. Why had the Indians come? was the question on every pair of lips.

"I guess they just wanted to look us over—see whether we mean any harm or not," said Mr Robertson.

"To see whether we've got any horses or cattle worth stealing, more like," grumbled someone.

"Should have shot them on the spot," said someone else. "The only good Injun is a dead Injun, I always say."

"That would have been the most foolish thing we could have done," said Uncle Seth quietly. "If we'd harmed them we'd have had the whole tribe of them down on us like a ton of bricks. I think Robertson is right. They just came to look us over, and we must keep on as friendly terms with them as we can."

"We can't afford not to," agreed Mr Robertson.

"This was their country first, after all, and you can't blame them for wondering why we've come here. Likely when they realise we're just travelling through they'll let us alone."

Everyone began to scatter to do the evening chores, to light their fires and cook their suppers.

Afterwards, when they were having their Bible reading and prayers, Ruth was surprised, because as well as praying for all their own people Uncle Seth prayed for the Indians, too. He prayed that all the Indians and white men would one day live together in peace and harmony and that all would worship and love the same God.

"Does God love Indians, too, then?" she asked as she got up to go to bed.

"He does," said Uncle Seth. "An Indian is a man, too, and God loves all men, whether their skins are white or brown, black or yellow. Sure, God loves Indians."

Ruth went to bed, feeling a little confused. Most people thought that Indians were savages, to be feared and avoided and killed. But they were only people trying to protect their own land. They could not help it if their ways and customs differed from ours. And God loved them. Uncle Seth said so.

Ruth thought of the little Indian papoose on the woman's back. She remembered its brown skin and black hair and bright eyes, and the peaceful way it slept bundled up on its mother's back. She thought of the way its mother had almost smiled when she saw the twins being dosed with medicine. Why, thought Ruth, the Indians are really not so very different from us. And she drifted off to sleep, feeling not even a little bit afraid.

CHAPTER ELEVEN

MOUNTAIN LION

The caravan of wagons rolled on. For a few days after the Indians had come the night watch was increased and more scouts patrolled on horseback by day, ready to warn of any possible danger. But no more was seen of the Indians, and the settlers hopefully decided that perhaps they need not fear trouble.

They came to a rough mountainous patch of country, a change from the miles and miles of prairie. Now it was hard going for the horses to pull their loads up the rough, steep slopes and through rocky passes. One day an axle broke and all the wagons waited while it was repaired. The women were glad of the chance to do some washing and ironing but the men were impatient and anxious to push on. They camped that night in a shallow valley, beside a little lake which had gathered from streams running down the mountainside.

When John came to breakfast next morning after doing the chores he had some bad news. During the night a half-grown heifer calf had disappeared. Neither of the two men on guard had heard or seen anything amiss.

"It could have wandered off and got caught by a bear or a lynx," said Uncle Seth. "Strange, though, that it should do that—there's not much grass here except round the lake."

It was true that there was not much grazing for the animals in this hilly area. Some of the cattle had bellowed with hunger during the night, but it seemed odd that one small heifer should wander off on her own. A hurried search was made but nothing could be found. Some of the men grumbled that the Indians had come back and stolen the heifer during the night. One or two even wanted to ride out after them, but the older and wiser farmers soon persuaded them of the foolishness of this idea. Better to lose one of the cattle than to start any trouble with the Indians.

The axle was mended and the wagons moved on, but the going was hard and they did not travel far that day. By nightfall they were still in the same mountain range, and that night four men instead of two guarded the camp in case whatever had taken the calf was still nearby.

Shortly after midnight a yell from one of the guards, followed by a shot, brought the others running and roused the whole camp. They found the man standing over another young calf, dying from vicious wounds and bites. A trail of blood leading up over the rocks into the mountain showed clearly in the moonlight. The guard said that he had seen a dark shape launch itself from the shadow of the rocks and attack the calf, and he had fired and wounded it, but it had escaped.

"It was a cougar—the biggest I've ever seen," said the man.

"Probably a mother with cubs—that'll be why it killed twice in two days," said someone else.

"It'll be dangerous now it's wounded," said the guard. "A wounded cougar is likely to attack anything —beast or man. We won't be safe in these mountains until it's killed."

It was decided that the cougar must be hunted and killed for the sake of the safety of everyone in the wagon train—humans as well as animals. A wounded mountain lion, maddened by pain, could stalk the camp and attack at any time.

So, early next morning the wagons rested while a well-armed party set out on the dangerous mission of seeking out and killing the cougar.

John was among the eight young men who made up the hunting party. Ruth's heart was in her mouth as she watched him ride off up the steep track with his gun over his saddle. How she hoped that no harm would come to him.

That day seemed very long. Ruth helped about the wagon and amused the twins. No-one must venture out of the circle of wagons because of the danger which might lurk in the mountains. As well as the wounded mountain lion there could well be bear, lynx or wolves. Ruth shuddered when she thought of all the eyes which could be watching them from dark lairs. She wished they were back on the safe, open prairie again.

But the long day came to an end at last, and at dusk there was the clatter of hooves on stony ground as the hunting party rode in triumphant. They had found where the wounded cougar was lying up, and had shot it quickly together with its half-grown cubs, and no-one had received so much as a scratch.

But Ruth saw at once that there were only seven horses and riders. "Oh, Aunt Susanna," she cried, "John hasn't come home!"

Aunt Susanna and Mary Rebecca were white-faced. But Uncle Seth, who had been talking to the hunters, quickly reassured them. "John's horse went a bit lame, and he fell back a little way," he said. "The others say he wasn't far behind—he should be here any minute."

They waited supper until John came, but half-an-hour later he still had not returned to camp. Puzzled, Uncle Seth and some of the young men quickly saddled up again and rode back to search for him. But when they came back John was not with them. They had retraced their route as far as they could before darkness fell, but had seen no trace of him or his horse.

Ruth burst into a storm of weeping. "Oh, he's dead! He's dead! The cougar has killed him. Oh, John! Oh, John!"

"For shame, Ruth—you will frighten the children," said Aunt Susanna firmly. "The cougar is dead—you know that. It cannot harm John."

But her face had a greyish tinge in the firelight, and there was an anxious question in her eyes as she looked at her husband. Uncle Seth put an arm round her shoulder, and the other round Ruth and Mary Rebecca who were holding hands tightly as though for comfort.

"I guess Beauty was lamer than we thought, and John couldn't ride her to the camp before dark," he said. "I think he'll curl up beside her in some sheltered spot for the night and come on home in the morning. The weather's warm, and he's got his gun. He'll be all right."

Ruth dried her eyes on her apron, feeling a little reassured and ashamed of her outburst. They were all silent as they tried to eat supper and afterwards went to bed in the wagon. David brought his bed in, too, and left the tent empty. When Ruth knelt to say her prayers she prayed for John as she had never prayed before, and hoped that God would hear. She knew that Uncle Seth and Aunt Susanna were praying too, and He would surely hear them.

But when she was in bed in the darkness, a great

wave of fear came over Ruth again. She thought of John all alone out there in the darkness, with snakes and bears and wolves and all sorts of awful things prowling around. A great sob rose in her throat, and she quickly put her head under the blankets to smother it. She must be brave, like Uncle Seth and Aunt Susanna and Mary Rebecca and David.

The night seemed very long, even longer than the day. Ruth slept only in snatches, waking in terror at some nightmare and remembering the real nightmare. Beside her Mary Rebecca tossed and turned, and sometimes a smothered sob came from her side of the bed. Ruth could tell from the way that they breathed that her aunt and uncle were not asleep either.

Aunt Susanna and Uncle Seth were up long before it was light, and many of the other pioneers were up and about too. At first light Uncle Seth and some others saddled up and rode off to begin another search. Some of the other wives came to stay with Aunt Susanna and the children while they waited. The wagons stayed still and everyone was silent and subdued.

The searchers came back just before noon, and this time they were leading Beauty by the bridle. They had found her wandering near some caves in the rocks, limping badly. But there had been no sign of John.

Uncle Seth looked worn and old. He said that they would search again, but if John was not found that day the wagon train must move on. They could not hold up the other pioneers for long. When Ruth heard him say that, she knew that Uncle Seth believed that John had been killed. She stood outside the wagon and tears ran like rain down her cheeks.

"Come inside," said Uncle Seth, and took them all into the wagon. He and Aunt Susanna were very calm.

They spoke gently to the children, telling them that perhaps John would not be coming back. Ruth sobbed and sobbed. Her heart felt as though it was broken in pieces. She wondered how her uncle and aunt could be so calm when such a dreadful thing had happened.

"Even if John is dead, he has not gone for ever," said Uncle Seth, as though he could read her thoughts. "All of us who love and trust the Lord Jesus will see him again one day in heaven."

"But I want to see him now," sobbed Ruth. "Oh, Uncle Seth, won't he come back?"

Uncle Seth looked very grave. "There are so many dangers when one is alone out here, Ruth. It may have been God's will to take him home to heaven, and God's way is always for the best. I guess if John comes back now it'll be a miracle."

Ruth's heart cried out in rebellion. A God who could take John like this could not be kind and loving. But all the same she could not help being impressed by the quiet faith and trust in God shown by her uncle and aunt.

The dreadful day came to an end, with more fruitless searches, and was followed by another long, sleepless night. The next day they were to move on, and they would never see John again. But as the camp began to stir in the first pale rays of the sun, the miracle happened. A figure came stumbling down the hillside towards the circle of wagons, and it was a human figure, and it was John.

CHAPTER TWELVE

JOHN AND THE BEAR

John was pale and weak and exhausted. He had had no food or drink since he had been away. There was a big, ugly bruise on his forehead, and his ankle was twisted. But he was alive and safe, and after he had eaten and drunk and rested he had a surprising tale to tell.

He said that he had been riding slowly along behind the others, taking things very easily because Beauty was a little lame and the ground was rocky and hard for her. Everyone was happy because the hunt had been successful and they were singing as they rode back into camp.

Then suddenly without warning Beauty stumbled on her lame leg and she fell forward on to her knees. John yelled as he was thrown over her head, but he thought the others had not heard because of their singing, as they had not missed him until they got to camp. As he reached the ground his head hit hard against a rocky outcrop, and he remembered no more for a time.

When he came to, it was dark and he was alone on the mountainside, lying in a patch of scrubby bushes. Beauty must have wandered off, because although the moon was shining he couldn't see her anywhere, or hear her. All around the rocks and trees made mysterious shapes, and there were little scufflings and rustlings of night creatures in the undergrowth. John could not remember how far away from the camp he was, but he thought it must be a long way because he could hear and see nothing of it. His gun had vanished with the horse and he was quite alone.

"Oh, John," said Ruth, her eyes round. "Weren't you afraid?"

"Well, I would rather have been sitting by the fire with a good supper inside me," admitted John.

"Only think—we must have ridden right past that patch of bushes while you were still unconscious," said Uncle Seth.

"I was buried good and deep in them," said John, and he showed the scratches on his face and arms to prove it.

"What did you do then?" asked David eagerly.

"Well, my ankle was twisted under me pretty badly and I didn't think I could make it home," said John. "I thought the best thing to do would be to find a bit of shelter and lie up there until it got light. I crawled along on my hands and knees, looking for an overhanging rock or some such to get under. But I was lucky—after a while I found a cave."

"And did you stay in it?" interrupted Ruth.

"Yes," said John. "There was a good screen of bushes in front of it, a bit of protection from wolves and suchlike, and a good, dry sandy floor. It smelled a bit, but I didn't mind that— I couldn't afford to be choosy. There was a sort of ledge along one wall, so I climbed up on that and lay down, and after a good while I went to sleep."

"But why didn't you come home in the morning?" wondered Aunt Susanna. "Was your ankle too bad still to walk on?"

"I guess my ankle would have made it all right," said John. "But when I woke up, I found I had company in the cave."

"Company?" squeaked Ruth and David together.

"Whatever do you mean?" asked Mary Rebecca.

"Well, I was woken by a sort of snuffling and grunting," said John. "It was getting light, and when I looked down from my ledge, what do you think? A great big fat old bear had come in and was curled up just inside the entrance, fast asleep. That cave must have been his lair, and he'd just come back for a snooze."

"Oh, John!" gasped Ruth.

"Whatever did you do?" asked Aunt Susanna.

"I just lay and waited," said John. "There wasn't much else I could do. That bear was right across the entrance; I'd have had to climb right over him to get out, and I didn't much fancy doing that. I made up my mind I'd just have to wait until he got hungry and went out looking for food again. But he must have had a real good feast before, because he lay there and slept all day long. He just got up and turned round once or twice, and sighed and snorted, and then went right back to sleep again. I heard you calling when you were searching for me, but I didn't dare shout for fear of waking him."

Ruth shuddered, to think of John shut up all that time with an awful bear.

"Strange how he didn't see you or smell you there in his lair," said one of the boys who had gone with John to hunt the cougar.

"Not so strange when you remember that we were praying," said Uncle Seth. "If God could shut the lions' mouths so that they didn't hurt Daniel, I guess he could stop a bear from knowing that John was in its cave with it. All the same, it was a narrow squeak."

"The strange thing is, I believe he did know I was there," said John. "All that second night I didn't dare go to sleep, because the bear was still there. I just had to lie on that ledge, all stiff and cramped, and hungry and thirsty, and my ankle throbbing fit to bust. Then as it was getting light again old Mr Bear decided it was time for breakfast. He got up and stretched and snuffled about a bit; then he ambled out through the bushes, and that was the last I saw of him. But just at the entrance he turned his head and looked straight at me, as much as to say, "Well, cheerio for now. It was nice knowing you!"

Everyone laughed, partly because of the funny way John told the tale and partly in relief that he was safely back. All the people from the other wagons kept coming over to hear his story. Ruth thought he was quite a hero. She couldn't do enough for him, fetching and carrying, helping Aunt Susanna to bind up his injured foot, and cooking especially nice things to feed him up. It was so wonderful to have him back safe and sound.

It was too late to hit the trail that day, but very early next morning the wagons were once again rumbling and creaking on their way. John sat beside his father at the front, resting his injured foot until it was well enough for him to ride again. Beauty's lameness was getting better, but it would do her good not to be ridden for a day or two.

In two more days they had left the mountains behind and were once again on open prairie land. There they could make better progress, and sometimes they travelled more than twenty miles in a day. The cattle could eat good grass again and the ground was softer to their worn and tired hooves. The weather kept fine and hot, the sky was blue, and plump yellow bumblebees buzzed above the prairie flowers. Ruth was happy. John had come back safe and she thought it would not be so very long before they were in Oregon.

CHAPTER THIRTEEN

THE EPIDEMIC

All day long Debbie had been restless and cross. She would not eat her food, would not play with her twin, her nose was runny and her skin felt hot to the touch. When someone picked her up she would push them away fretfully. Aunt Susanna had been worried about her all day, and when they made camp she told Uncle Seth that perhaps the doctor should look at her.

A doctor was travelling with the wagons, a young man just qualified who had decided to come West with the pioneers. After the chores John, whose ankle was almost well now, went to the wagon where the doctor lived, and asked him to come.

Ruth liked young Doctor Rivers. He looked not much older than John, and had fair hair falling like a thatch over his forehead; he was kind and nice and people said he was very clever. He got Debbie to sit very quietly on his knee in the wagon while he listened to her chest and looked into her mouth and ears and down her throat. When he had finished he tucked her up in bed again, and went outside to talk to Aunt Susanna and Uncle Seth.

"I think she has chicken-pox," he said. "Unless I am very much mistaken she will come out in spots in the next few days. She already has one or two on her back."

"Chicken-pox?" said Aunt Susanna. "But where can she have caught chicken-pox? We have been on the trail for weeks, and no-one else has it."

Dr Rivers shook his head. He didn't know where

the chicken-pox could have come from, only that it was there! He left a soothing mixture for Debbie and went back to his wagon, promising to come again in the morning.

"I think he must be mistaken," said Aunt Susanna as she made Debbie comfortable for the night. "I don't think she can have got chicken-pox. Perhaps it's just heat rash."

But Dr Rivers was not mistaken. The very next morning Debbie was covered in pinkish spots, some already forming blisters—as fine a case of chicken-pox as Aunt Susanna had ever seen. The doctor gave her more medicine and instructions about how to nurse Debbie, which Aunt Susanna didn't really need as she was an excellent nurse. However, she thanked him politely and said to Uncle Seth afterwards that it was a great comfort to have a doctor travelling with them.

For a day or two poor little Debbie had a miserable time of it. She lay in bed in the jolting wagon, feverish, itching and spotty. Then the worst was over and she began to feel better. Dr Rivers and Aunt Susanna both agreed that it was fortunate that her illness was chicken-pox and not a more serious one like measles.

But by this time David was feeling off-colour, and in a day or two he also had a fine chicken-pox rash. Aunt Susanna moved him from the tent and put him to bed in the wagon. Then two children in another wagon came out in spots, and then the Robertsons' little girl. In a few days chicken-pox was spreading through the wagon-train like wildfire, and almost every family had at least one sick child. The wagons made camp beside a river and waited for the epidemic to die down. It was not fair to keep on travelling with so many itching, irritable children.

In the Carey wagon Ruth was having a busy time. Of the children, John was the only one who had had chicken-pox before. A few days after David, Daniel came out in spots and was put to bed beside his twin. Next day Mary Rebecca was sick too. Everyone expected Ruth to catch chicken-pox as well, but so far she had not. All day long she was busy helping Aunt Susanna to look after the others, fetching and carrying for them, helping to apply the starch solution which eased the itching, amusing the little ones and trying to keep them from scratching, and fetching endless drinks of water. At night she sank into bed exhausted.

But at last the worst seemed to be over and the Carey children were getting better. One by one they emerged, pale and spotty, and then they began to get dressed and lead a normal life again. Most of the other children were getting better too, but one family was not so fortunate, for their baby had developed rare complications. The poor little mite had ear-ache and cried day and night with the pain. Even Dr Rivers could not relieve it, and its parents were almost out of their minds with worry and weariness.

One afternoon Aunt Susanna said she would go over and see if there was anything she could do. Now that her own family were convalescent she spent a great deal of time going round the other families, doing what she could to help and advise. She was a welcome visitor in every wagon because she was kind and calm and full of commonsense.

"Ruth, will you stay in the wagon and keep an eye on Daniel?" asked Aunt Susanna, and Ruth said that she would. Uncle Seth and John were out hunting for some fresh meat. Mary Rebecca, David and Debbie had been sent out to walk on the prairie to get some air into their lungs and colour in their cheeks. Only Daniel was not allowed out yet, because he still had some spots.

Ruth sat beside him in the wagon. It was the end of June now and very hot, and both ends of the wagon cover were rolled back to let the air blow through. Daniel was tired of being cooped up in the wagon. He wanted to go out and play, and shrieked when Ruth would not let him. Her head ached and she felt shivery, in spite of the heat, but she sat patiently and built houses of blocks for him to knock down.

"Sing!" he demanded when he grew tired of that game. So Ruth sang all the nursery rhymes she could think of. 'Ding dong, bell, pussy's in the well' was his favourite, and he made her sing it over and over again. But at last his golden head drooped, and he curled up in a little ball on the bed and went to sleep.

Ruth sighed with relief. She felt hot and sticky now instead of shivery. She went and sat on the front of the wagon so that she could feel the breeze. Not many people were about the camp. Most of the children who were better or who had not been ill had gone to play on the prairie or in a shallow place in the river just below where the wagons were. Ruth leaned her head on her arms and dozed a little.

She woke suddenly with a start. Her head was still aching and she felt a little confused. Was it time to start getting the supper things ready yet? No, it could not be. Aunt Susanna was not back yet from visiting that poor little baby.

She turned her head to see if Daniel was still asleep, and her eyes suddenly flew wide open with astonishment. The little boy was not there.

She saw the rumpled bed, with the dent in it where he had been lying, she saw the building blocks on the floor. The breeze blew softly through the opening at the back and the afternoon sun shone in, making a wide strip of brightness along the length of the wagon. But it was quite empty. Daniel had gone.

CHAPTER FOURTEEN

THE RIVER BANK HOLE

Ruth scrambled back into the wagon and looked out through the opening. She saw at once what must have happened. Daniel had wakened and, finding Ruth half asleep at the front, had cunningly taken the opportunity to escape and had climbed out over the feed-box to the ground. He was nowhere in sight. Ruth climbed to the ground herself, her headache forgotten. She must find Daniel quickly before any harm came to him. Calling his name, she looked under the wagon and into the tent, but there was no sign of the small boy. Oh, where could he have gone? There was no-one about the nearest wagons. Should she run for Aunt Susanna? But there was no time for that; the wagon she had gone to was right at the other end of camp, and anything could happen to Daniel while she ran all that way and back. She could see Mary Rebecca and the other two, little dots far away on the prairie, far out of calling distance. There was no-one to help. She must find her little cousin herself.

Ruth looked desperately around, and then she saw Robert Snow standing near his family's wagon, pale and a little spotty because he had had chicken-pox, too. He had been watching her all the time. Ruth did not like him and she knew he had never forgiven her and David for playing tricks on him at the first camp; but surely he would help. She ran up to him.

"Oh, Robert, I've lost Daniel," she cried desperately. "Have you seen him?"

The big boy shrugged at first, then he pointed upriver away from the camp. "He ran off that way," he muttered.

Ruth's heart almost stopped. There were high banks to the river up there, over which a little child could easily fall if he went too near.

"Oh, why didn't you stop him?" she said, and she began to run in that direction. She wished with all her heart that she had never made fun of Robert Snow. Then perhaps he wouldn't have been so mean as to let her little cousin run off alone into danger.

"Tell Aunt Susanna," she yelled back over her shoulder as she ran. Her heart pounded and her lungs seemed near bursting as she raced towards the creek. There was a clump of willows on the first bend, and she thought perhaps Daniel was playing among them. When she reached the trees he was not there, but as she emerged from them she saw a tiny white figure on the bank further upstream. She felt a surge of relief. At least he had not fallen in the river.

"Daniel!" she called breathlessly, still running. "Daniel, wait for me."

The little boy looked over his shoulder and saw his cousin coming running. His face split into an impish grin.

"Can't catch me," he squeaked gleefully, and he began to run as fast as his plump bare legs would carry him. He looked over his shoulder and laughed and squealed at the sight of Ruth chasing him. And he was heading straight for the edge of the bank, with its steep drop into the river.

"Daniel, Daniel, stop!" screamed Ruth frantically, redoubling her efforts. But he took no notice. He had no sense of danger, and this was a great game, much better than staying in the wagon!

Ruth's head swam, but with one last effort she flung

herself forward and grabbed at Daniel's little white nightgown just as he reached the very edge of the bank. He screamed in protest but she yanked him back firmly, feeling faint with relief.

Ruth did not quite know what happened next. One moment she was standing holding Daniel in the long grass on the brink of the river; the next moment the ground seemed to give way beneath her feet, and they were both falling. They landed with a thump on soft earth, with Daniel on top of Ruth, and for a moment all the breath seemed knocked out of her body. Then she gathered her senses together and tried to scramble up.

But she could not. They had fallen through a thin layer of earth on top of the bank, right into a hole dug out of the bank itself. It had probably once been the home of some river animal but it was deserted now. There was just room for them to sit huddled up as they were now. A small hole in front of them opened right on to the flowing water of the river, and far above was the other hole they had fallen through, thickly covered by long prairie grass.

Daniel was screaming and tightly clinging to his cousin. He was not hurt but frightened and bewildered by their sudden fall. Ruth tried to calm him, but she was badly shaken herself and for a few moments could not collect her confused thoughts. When she stood in the hole she was still a long way from the top. She could not even reach the top when she stretched her arms to their full length. The sides were made of crumbly earth; it was impossible to get a foothold or handhold or to climb up. And the only other way out was the hole which opened on to the deep, swift-flowing river.

As Daniel's screams faded to little hiccups and

snuffles, slow realisation dawned upon Ruth. There was no way they could get out! They were trapped in this damp, chilly little hole in the river bank into which they had fallen.

For a moment panic surged over her. She wanted to shout and scream, to jump out into the water; anything to get out of this dreadful cramped prison. Then she calmed a little. Robert Snow knew which direction they had come and he would tell the others. When Aunt Susanna and Uncle Seth found they were missing they would come to look for them, and would rescue them. She sat down as comfortably as she could on the earth floor, took Daniel on her lap and settled down to wait.

It seemed a long time that they sat there, looking out at the water flowing past. The sunlight glinted on it, making little points and sparkles of light. The only sound to be heard was the gurgle and chuckle of the flowing water.

Then at last voices could be heard, sounding very faint and far away. But they were voices. Ruth jumped up and shouted and yelled and screeched, "Uncle Seth! We're here! Uncle Seth, John! Uncle Seth!" Daniel yelled too, although he did not know why. They both shouted and screamed until they were hoarse.

When Ruth paused for breath she was sure that they must have been heard, and that soon they would see the grasses being parted at the top of the hole and Uncle Seth's face looking down. But the grasses just waved gently as before, completely covering up their prison. Even the voices could no longer be heard. Ruth shouted again until she could shout no more. But still no-one came. The deep, earthy walls had such a muffling effect that no sound could be heard from above. And no-one would even guess at the existence of a hole under the thick grass on the edge of the bank.

Dusk was beginning to fall as at last Ruth gave up and sank to the floor again. She and Daniel clung together and sobbed until at last the little boy fell asleep from sheer exhaustion. Ruth cuddled him close and looked out over the darkening water. An owl hooted on the opposite bank, and she knew night was coming. And they would have to spend it here in this prison, all alone in the darkness. It would be a long night, but surely in the morning they would be found.

CHAPTER FIFTEEN

RESCUED

Up on the prairie the summer night was hot, but in the hole beside the river a chilliness came from the damp earth walls. Daniel woke in a panic and cried because it was dark and he was frightened and hungry and thirsty. Ruth comforted him as best she could. She kneeled forward and dipped her cupped hands through the river opening, scooping up some water for him to drink, and afterwards drank herself. At least they would not go thirsty.

Daniel shivered as a few drips of water trickled down his neck. He only had on his thin summer nightgown, and Ruth was worried in case he caught cold. Quickly she unbuttoned her dress and pulled it over her head. She wrapped the folds of calico round the little boy and cuddled him in her arms.

"Is that better, Daniel?" she asked and he said sleepily, "Yes."

Soon he had fallen asleep again. Ruth rested his weight as comfortably as she could across her knees and tried to sleep too. But she could not. The cold crept in through her thin petticoats and she shivered, although her face burned feverishly. Her bare feet felt like stones. Oh, if only she had watched Daniel and looked after him, they would not be trapped in this hateful place.

She thought of the snug wagon and wondered what the family were doing. Were they still looking for them, or had they given up because of the dark? And would they find them in the morning, or would she and Daniel be left to starve to death by the river?

Ruth put her face down on to Daniel's golden curls and sobbed quietly. She remebered the night when John was lost, and how they had prayed, and how calm Aunt Susanna and Uncle Seth were. They had known that if John died they would see him again one day. Could they say the same about her? Ruth's heart felt it would break with despair when she remembered that first Sunday on the trail. Uncle Seth had asked her if she would receive Jesus as her Saviour, and she had not. And now it was too late.

But was it too late? Suddenly into Ruth's mind leapt a Bible verse she and Mary Rebecca had learned for Sunday school many months ago: 'Him that cometh to me I will in no wise cast out.' She knew that Jesus had said that, and that everything Jesus said could be depended upon. Could she come to Him here by the river and ask Him to forgive her and make her one of His children? She felt that she could. Quickly she closed her eyes, folded her hands around Daniel and began to pray. For the first time she felt she was really talking to God, not just reciting words as she had done before when she prayed. She told God how sorry she was that she had turned her back on Him, and thanked Him for sending Jesus to die on the cross for her sins. She asked that Jesus would come into her heart and forgive her. Then she prayed for Uncle Seth and Aunt Susanna and all the family, and asked that Daniel and she might be found.

When she had finished she was still cold and stiff and cramped but there was a peace somewhere deep inside her that hadn't been there before. She had put herself into God's hands, and whatever happened now would be according to His will. This was such a comforting thought that she smiled to herself in the darkness. She dried her tears on her petticoat, and hugged the sleeping child. Her head still ached and her throat was sore, but soon her eyes closed and she slept.

When Ruth awoke it was getting light. Streaks of sunlight were glinting on the water and reflecting into the dark hole. She shivered, shifted Daniel's weight and tried to stretch her cramped limbs. The little boy slept, warm and snug in his calico wrapper. He looked as peaceful as though he was in his own little bed.

Ruth wondered how long it would be before someone came searching again. They must shout loud enough this time so that they would be heard.

She sat looking at the swirling water and waiting. Bits of grass and twigs floated down. Then a whole willow branch swirled into view and caught against the bank of the river. It rocked there gently, one end of it fast against a bit of the bank that stuck out.

Ruth had a sudden idea. If she could get that branch, perhaps it would be long enough to reach up through the top of the hole. She could tie something on to it and wave it about, and surely someone would see. She laid Daniel down beside her carefully without waking him and bent forward over the water. She had to lean far out to reach the branch, and as she did so a piece of the earth went plopping down into the water, but she was safe, and she had the branch.

Daniel woke as she drew it dripping into the hole. He did not seem surprised to find himself there, and asked Ruth what she was doing.

"I'm making a flag," she told him. "A flag to rescue us."

She bundled the little boy out of his wrappings and quickly put on her dress. She could only reach to do up some of the buttons, and Daniel's fingers were too small, but it didn't matter. It was light now, and the camp must surely be astir. She picked up her crumpled apron and tried it by its strings to the willow branch. Then she pushed the stick up towards the hole with the apron-flag at the top. She saw with relief that it was long enough to reach the opening and go through. She stood and waved the flag back and forth with all her might.

For a long time nothing happened. Ruth's arms grew tired and she pulled the branch down to rest for a while. But soon she pushed it up again and waved it about. She must keep the flag flying in case anyone happened to be looking in that direction. Then she heard voices, sounding very faint and far away, as they had the night before. They came nearer.

"Uncle Seth!" shouted Ruth. Her voice came out hoarse and croaking, but she shouted again and again. "Uncle Seth! Uncle Seth! We're here!"

Daniel shouted too, and all the time Ruth waved the branch with the apron tied on top for all that she was worth. Her throat ached with shouting, her arms and shoulders from holding the branch, but she didn't give up for a moment.

Then suddenly she could stop. The voices had come very near until they were right overhead, and then the grasses at the top of the hole were parting, and Uncle Seth's brown face with the bristly, black beard was looking down at them with relief and amazement and joy.

All at once Ruth could not stand up. Her legs trembled, her eyes blurred, and she dropped the stick and fell in a heap beside Daniel. She was hardly conscious of the hustle and bustle as men brought ropes and climbed down and brought up Daniel and herself. She was only dimly aware of Uncle Seth carrying her home and Aunt Susanna putting her to bed in the wagon and feeding her with hot broth. Then she slept.

Mary Rebecca was sitting beside her when she awoke, sewing a neat patch on a pair of John's trousers. She put down the sewing and leaned over Ruth when she saw that her cousin was awake.

"Do you want anything, Ruth?" she asked, and when Ruth said, "A drink, please," she brought a cup of water and held it while she drank. Mary Rebecca's hand trembled slightly and there were dark circles under her eyes.

"Oh, Ruth," she said shakily, "I'm so glad you're back safe. We all thought you'd both been drowned in the river. Oh it was awful!"

Tears shone in her blue eyes and Ruth was touched. She had not realised that Mary Rebecca cared so much about her.

"What time is it?" she asked, and Mary Rebecca said, "It's past three. You've slept for nine hours. Daniel slept for a long time too, but Mother's taken him out now so as not to disturb you."

Ruth struggled to sit up. She did not feel very well but it was time she got up.

"Where are my clothes?" she asked.

"Oh, but you can't get up," said Mary Rebecca. "You'll be in bed for at least a few days."

She rose quickly and got her mother's looking-glass from the box where she kept her things, and held it in front of Ruth's face. "Don't you know what's the matter with you?" she said.

Ruth looked, and saw her own face, pale and covered all over with a pinkish spotty rash. In a flash realisation dawned. She had chicken-pox!

CHAPTER SIXTEEN

LEFT BEHIND

At first having chicken-pox was rather fun. Everyone fell over themselves waiting on Ruth hand and foot and being kind to her. David told her everything that was going on outside, and John and Mary Rebecca took it in turns to read aloud to her. People came from the other wagons to visit and sometimes brought little gifts. All the choicest morsels of food were saved for her, and Aunt Susanna cooked special dishes.

Daniel was none the worse for his night out, and everyone said that it was because Ruth had wrapped him in her dress and kept him warm. But the very best thing of all was telling Uncle Seth and Aunt Susanna of the prayer she had prayed by the river, and how Jesus was now her Saviour, too. When she saw the look of joy and thankfulness on their faces she felt that she would cheerfully go through that awful night all over again.

Almost all the other children in the camp were better from the chicken-pox, and the wagons were preparing to move on. Soon they would be on their way again, and Ruth would be up and about. But instead of feeling better, Ruth began to feel worse. Her spots were fading but she had developed a persistent cough. All night long it kept her awake, and every time she coughed her chest hurt. In the morning Aunt Susanna looked worried. She touched Ruth's hot, sweaty forehead and murmured to Uncle Seth, "I think someone had better fetch Dr Rivers."

By the time the doctor came Ruth felt too ill to

greet him. She tossed and turned on the bed, sweaty and hot one moment and shivering the next. The pain in her chest stabbed her every time she coughed. She was dimly aware of Dr Rivers pulling back the bedclothes and listening to her chest. Then he covered her up and went away to talk to the grown-ups.

She heard odd words and snatches of conversation, spoken in serious tones: 'the left lung', 'pneumonia', and 'that night in the open', but she was too ill to really listen. Then someone was giving her something bitter which made her cough yet again, and she was drifting off into a restless sleep.

After that everything seemed a blur. Sometimes Ruth slept fitfully, sometimes she was awake and tossed and turned on the bed. Sometimes it was daylight in the wagon, sometimes it was night and a lamp burned. Faces came and went—anxious faces—Aunt Susanna and Uncle Seth, Dr Rivers, sometimes Mary Rebecca and John. They spoke to her and sometimes she tried to answer, but the words somehow wouldn't come out right. And always there was the cough, the endless cough which racked her body with burning pain.

Then came a night when her mind was suddenly clear. She saw that all the faces were around the bed, and wondered why they all seemed so haggard and worn and sad. Aunt Susanna had tears in her eyes, and more tears were pouring down Mary Rebecca's cheeks. But she was too tired to think about it. Her eyes were closing and she felt herself drifting far away.

It seemed a long, long time later when Ruth opened her eyes. Daylight streamed in through the open front of the wagon and Aunt Susanna sat sewing beside the bed. Ruth watched her aunt's face. It seemed somehow thinner and older, and there were some grey streaks in her hair which Ruth was sure she had not noticed before. Her eyes looked strained, and she screwed them up wearily as she sewed.

"Oh, Aunt Susanna, you do look tired," said Ruth. Her voice came out sounding very thin and weak, but Aunt Susanna jumped as though she had shouted the words. She dropped the sewing and got up, bending low over Ruth.

"Ruth, dear, how are you feeling?" she asked with a glad smile, pushing back the tumbled hair from Ruth's forehead.

Ruth considered for a moment. She felt very weak and tired, and somehow as though she had been a long way away. But the fever and sweating and pain had gone, and her skin was cool. And she hardly felt like coughing at all.

"I'm hungry," she said at last, and her aunt smiled and bent to kiss her. "Just lie still. I'll fetch some hot soup."

She bustled out of the wagon to the camp fire, calling her daughter. Mary Rebecca appeared from outside and sat down where her mother had been.

"I'm so glad you're better," she said, and Ruth knew that she meant it.

"Have I been very ill, then?" she asked wonderingly.

"Why, I should say so," said her cousin. "You've had pneumonia and we all thought you were going to die. Dr Rivers thought so too, but after the crisis you went to sleep and you've slept a whole night and almost a whole day. Dr Rivers says you'll get better now, and Father thinks it is a miracle."

"Fancy that," said Ruth weakly. Her aunt came back with the soup and fed it to her with a spoon because her own hand was too shaky to hold it. She sponged Ruth with warm water and popped a clean nightgown over her head.

"Now go to sleep again, if you can," she said.

Ruth certainly could. In fact she felt that she could not have stayed awake if she tried.

Next time she woke it was the usual time for getting up. The children were chattering outside and Aunt Susanna's pans were clattering as she prepared breakfast. Mary Rebecca was in the wagon just doing up the last button on Debbie's pinafore.

"What day is it?" asked Ruth, trying to sit up. She managed it at last but her head whirled so much that she was glad to lie down again.

"It's Friday," said Mary Rebecca.

"Friday!" said Ruth in surprise. "Then I've been ill for four whole days!"

"Four days!" exclaimed Mary Rebecca. "You have been ill for more than two weeks! It's the third week of July."

Ruth was astonished. She sat up again, and this time her head did not whirl and she stayed sitting up. How could so much time have passed by while she was lying there in the wagon? It seemed only a day or two since she and Daniel had spent that night in the river bank hole.

"Don't fret about it," said Mary Rebecca kindly. "I'll fetch your breakfast."

When she came back with hot cornmeal mush and milk Ruth was suddenly ravenous. She took the spoon and ate up every speck, feeling stronger every moment. Aunt Susanna beamed when she came in and saw the empty bowl.

"We'll have you well in no time at all," she said cheerfully.

Something seemed different about the wagon, and

suddenly Ruth realised what it was. It was too quiet outside. There were the soft voices of the family talking as they ate their breakfasts, there were prairie birds singing and the river softly babbling not far away, but that was all. There was none of the loud voices, shouting, clattering and lowing of cattle which usually heralded a new day in camp.

"Why is everything so still?" she asked, puzzled.

The cheerfulness went from Aunt Susanna's face. She sat down suddenly as she had when the Indians went away. She did not answer for a moment and Ruth wondered whatever could be the matter.

"I guess you may as well know," said her aunt at last. "You were ill so long, you see, and you had to be kept quiet and not moved. The wagons were all ready to move on, and your uncle felt we couldn't keep holding them back just because of us. So he told them to go on, and we'd catch them up if we could. Dr Rivers stayed until the crisis, but he had to ride after the wagons then because Mrs Wilding is expecting her baby any time now. They've been gone nearly two weeks. We're all on our own."

CHAPTER SEVENTEEN

MOVING ON

Ruth stared at her aunt in dismay. This was dreadful news!

"Oh, Aunt Susanna," she gasped. "We must catch up with them! Quick, tell Uncle Seth to hitch up right away and start now. We can't get left behind or we'll never get to Oregon."

She flung back the bedclothes as if to climb out of bed, and the sudden movement set off a fit of coughing. At once Aunt Susanna was beside her, pushing her back gently and smoothing her forehead with a cool hand.

"There, there, Ruthie," she soothed, tucking in the covers again. "We'll start off just as soon as you're well enough, be sure we will. But you aren't fit to travel yet a while."

"Oh, it's all my fault," wailed Ruth.

"Of course it's not," said her aunt firmly. "You couldn't help getting ill. And we're so glad you got better, that we didn't mind getting left behind. Now lie still and don't you fret and worry. Everything will be fine."

She bustled away, leaving Ruth alone in the wagon.

Ruth lay down again, feeling miserable. It was dreadful to be left behind! How would they ever manage to catch up with the other wagons? If they did not they would find it almost impossible to reach Oregon, she thought. And Uncle Seth did so want to get to Oregon! She closed her eyes and lay still, willing herself to get well as soon as possible.

She was so weak and thin that it was almost another week before she could get out of bed and walk about, wrapped in a shawl. At first her legs felt strange and wobbly and her head swam. But she was determined, and the feeling wore off. It was a great day when Aunt Susanna said she could get dressed and come outside to have dinner by the fire with the others.

How strange and bright and unfamiliar the grass and the sky and the river seemed! Ruth had to screw up her eyes tightly at first because they were not used to the strong sunlight after being so long in the dim wagon. But it was wonderful to gaze across the limitless prairie and see the buffalo grass waving and feel the breeze against her face again.

The camping place looked bare now that everyone else had gone. There were lighter patches in the grass where the other wagons had stood, and charred spots where their fires had burned. But now there was only their own wagon and tent, and the horses and Polly tethered to graze nearby.

John had shot two cottontails, and Aunt Susanna had made them into a delicious rabbit stew with potatoes and herbs. As they sat down to eat it Ruth said suddenly, "Oh, Uncle Seth, when can we start after the others? I'm well now, truly I am. Can we go tomorrow?"

"Well now, Scatterbrain," said Uncle Seth with a twinkle. "I won't argue that you're getting well—anyone can tell that by the amount you eat! But about moving on—well, I don't know. I guess we should all have a talk about that." Everyone looked at him. He spoke as cheerfully as usual, but in spite of the twinkle there was somehow a sad look in his eyes.

"What do you mean, Seth?" asked Aunt Susanna quickly.

Her husband laid down his spoon. "Well, I've been thinking that perhaps we'd do better to stay here over the winter," he said. "The others are nearly a month ahead of us, and we cannot hope to catch them up now. There are three or four families of settlers living in log cabins about a mile down the river. John and I met them out hunting one day and I've spoken to them several times since. They're keen for us to build ourselves a cabin and settle here for a while. We could hunt and trap and maybe trade furs this winter. Then when the good weather comes in the spring we could finish the journey to Oregon."

Everyone was silent for a moment. Then Ruth burst out, "But, Uncle Seth—you must be in Oregon in the spring to plant next year's crops!"

In a moment everyone was talking at once. John and David wanted to move on to Oregon now, to be there in time for the spring planting, Mary Rebecca liked the prairie and wanted to stay there for the winter. Aunt Susanna liked the prairie too, but she said that Uncle Seth must do just as he thought best. Uncle Seth held up his hand for silence.

"There is another reason why it might be best to stay," he said slowly, "and that's on account of the Indians. James Day—that's one of the settlers—is expecting possible trouble from them. He thinks it would not be safe for us to travel alone through hostile Indian country. Much safer for all concerned if we joined up with the other families and stayed here, just in case there is any trouble."

"But the Cheyennes are peaceful," protested John. "They intended us no harm when they came to the camp that time, and they haven't bothered us since."

"But things have changed since then," said Uncle Seth. "Day says he has heard a rumour that a Cheyenne brave was shot by a white man not long ago, and naturally the Indians won't take that lying down. Some of them have a camp over there." He pointed to the South-West. "On a still night Day can hear them from his cabin, and these last few nights he's heard a lot of singing and shouting and dancing going on. He thinks they may be planning to go on the warpath."

Ruth felt a thrill of excitement tingle down her spine. David and Mary Rebecca were staring round-eyed at their father.

"So," Uncle Seth went on, "we have to decide whether to go on and perhaps meet up with hostile Indians, or whether to stay with the other settlers where we'd be safer. Day has been on friendly terms with the Cheyennes and thinks they wouldn't attack his settlement."

"Well, Seth," said Aunt Susanna calmly and cheerfully, "you must decide for us. I know you will do what is best."

Uncle Seth threw her a look of love and gratitude. "Thank you, Susanna," he said. "I have prayed much about this, and I feel that the Lord is leading us to go on to Oregon. If He wants us to get there, then we'll get there whatever the risks. But if any of you would rather stay, then we'll stay."

"Let's go on," said John and David together, almost in one breath, and Ruth echoed excitedly, "Oh, yes, let's go on to Oregon!" Even Mary Rebecca nodded in agreement, and the twins piped up "Go on, go on," although they did not understand what it was all about. Aunt Susanna looked at her husband over their heads. "It's as you say, Seth. The Lord will take care of us," she said.

So two days later they set off again on their journey. It had rained the night before and the prairie looked green and fresh. The horses were fit and fresh after their long rest, and everyone was in good spirits. Even the thought of Indians could not get them down. It was good to be hitting the trail again.

They passed the little settlement beside the river which Uncle Seth had spoken about. There were four or five little square log cabins with smoke curling from the chimneys. Uncle Seth stopped to have a word with James Day, a tall, brown-haired man who came to the door of one of the cabins. A fair-haired woman followed him to the doorway, while a swarm of four or five little blonde children came spilling out to stare open-mouthed at the wagon.

James Day shook his head when he heard that they were moving on. "Well, I can't make you stay," he said. "But I wish you would, all the same. I'd gladly help build a cabin for you and share all I have with you and yours."

Uncle Seth thanked him but said that they would press on as fast as they could to try to reach Oregon before the winter. The two men shook hands as they set off again, and all the children waved until the log cabins looked like doll's houses far away in the distance.

CHAPTER EIGHTEEN

INDIAN PAPOOSE

They travelled twenty miles that day and even further the next. The countryside was changing slightly, and now seemed more like desert than prairie. The soil was sandy and sometimes it was difficult to find water to camp by. On the fourth night no creek or river could be found, but by a stroke of good fortune they discovered something even better—a clear spring which gushed out from under a large rock and disappeared into a hole in the ground.

"Now, Ruth, into bed right away," said Aunt Susanna almost before the wagon had stopped. "I'll bring your supper in as soon as it's ready."

But Ruth was tired of being mollycoddled. She was feeling so much better that she wanted to run through the grass again, to jump and shout and make up for all the time she had missed.

"Oh, Aunt Susanna, please mayn't I just walk a little bit," she pleaded. "Just as far as the spring and back. I could fetch the water. I'll come straight back, truly I will."

"Well, all right," Aunt Susanna relented. "But afterwards, into bed. You have to rest and get your strength back."

Ruth got the water pail and ran off to the spring. She cupped her hands and let the water gush into them, and drank. How cool and clear and delicious it was! She would have liked to paddle her dusty feet in the sparkling water but she did not dare. Aunt

Susanna would be cross if she did not go straight back as she had promised.

Ruth had just filled the pail when suddenly a most peculiar sensation crept over her. She was sure that she was not alone, that eyes were watching her movements. She whirled round from the water and screamed shrilly. Six Indians on ponies stood round the spring in a semi-circle, looking silently at her. They had ridden up so softly on the sandy soil that she had not noticed them coming.

Ruth put down her pail and her hands flew to her mouth, stifling another scream. The Indians watched her silently. Five of them were men, strong and brown, with impassive faces and feathered, black scalp-locks. They carried guns. The sixth was the woman who had come into their wagon, and she had her baby on her back. Their ponies were beautiful, piebald black and grey and white, with flowing manes and tails. They stood quietly, waiting for a command from their masters.

Ruth glanced at the camp, her eyes wide with terror. Only Aunt Susanna and the children were there, out of sight as they tended the fire round the other side of the wagon. Uncle Seth and John had gone off to hunt meat for tomorrow. Ruth could not warn them that the Indians had come. And if they were warned, what could they do? They were unarmed and helpless.

For a long moment the six strong brown faces stared at Ruth's small white one. Then one of the men moved his horse out of the way and motioned her to go to the wagon. She picked up the water pail and walked on shaking legs, and the Indians touched their ponies with their heels and followed. Not a word had been spoken.

The faces of Aunt Susanna, Mary Rebecca and

David turned towards them in horror as Ruth and the Indians came into camp. Sam snarled and would have lunged forward, but David quickly caught him by the collar and held him fast. The twins ran to their mother and hid their faces in her skirt. Ruth thought she would have liked to do the same. But she stood still on trembling legs and wondered what was going to happen.

One of the Indian men and the woman dismounted. The woman took her baby from her back, bundle and all, and held it in her arms. She walked towards the wagon and climbed into it. The man, who seemed to be her husband, said something in his own language and motioned Aunt Susanna to follow.

"Don't move or say anything—and hang on to Sam," she said quickly to the children as she did so.

From where she stood beside the fire Ruth could see clearly into the wagon. The Indian woman was looking about her. Her eye fell on the box where Aunt Susanna kept her coffee and sugar, her flour, spices and herbs. She made a motion of opening it, and Aunt Susanna did so. The woman looked at the contents and said something that Ruth could not understand. Aunt Susanna shook her head to show that she could not understand, either. Ruth wondered what it could be that the woman wanted.

Now the Indian squaw was unwrapping her baby and showing it to Aunt Susanna. It began to cry, a miserable wailing sound. Ruth could see its little face above the blanket. Its dark eyes were no longer bright but dull and lustreless, its nose was runny and its brown skin was covered with a familiar rash. The little Indian papoose had chicken-pox!

Its mother gestured to the baby, then pointed again at the box, and suddenly Ruth realised what it was she wanted. She had remembered the medicine she had seen being given to the twins, and how they had quickly seemed to get well afterwards. She wanted it to cure her baby's chicken-pox. Aunt Susanna understood too, for she quickly reached into the box and took out a little package of dried herbs and handed it to the woman. The Indian squaw took it but did not seem to be quite satisfied. She pointed again to her baby, then pointed away across the prairie towards where the Indian camp was, and made a sweeping gesture with her arm. Ruth did not know what she meant, but it seemed that Aunt Susanna did. She was taking out all the medicines and herbs she had and giving them to the Indian woman. Then she held out her empty hands, palm up, to show that that was all she had.

The squaw seemed satisfied. She put all the little packages away inside her blanket and climbed out of the wagon. She turned and said one more thing to Aunt Susanna, then climbed on to her pony, swinging her baby on to her back. Her husband mounted silently and they all rode away.

Aunt Susanna was shaking as she climbed out of the wagon. The twins ran to her and she sat down and hugged them for a while as she recovered. Sam was still growling as he looked after the departing riders, and David tied him to the wagon wheel for safety.

"You were good children to stay still and quiet," said Aunt Susanna at last. "One wrong move and we might all have been killed. But it was all right," she added, seeing the girls' frightened faces; "they only wanted medicine for that poor baby."

She got up and started to prepare supper as usual, and everyone began to breathe more freely. Next moment Uncle Seth and John came galloping into the camp. They had seen the Indians riding away and were relieved to see that everyone was safe. Aunt Susanna quickly explained what had happened.

"You did right to give them what they wanted," Uncle Seth nodded approvingly.

"What did she mean when she waved her arm and pointed away to their camp?" wondered Mary Rebecca.

"I think she meant that a lot of the Indian children are sick too, and she wanted more medicine for all of them," said Aunt Susanna. "How strange that the Indians should get chicken-pox, too. I suppose they haven't seen it before and don't believe any of their cures are any good for it."

"I hope all your potions will do them some good," said Uncle Seth. "And I guess I know where our children caught chicken-pox from. Likely some of the Indians had it about them when they came into our camp that first time."

"There's one good thing," said John. "If a lot of their children are sick they might think twice about going on the warpath."

This was a cheering thought. Ruth's heart was beating almost normally again, and Uncle Seth was back so she felt safe. Perhaps the Indians would not trouble them again.

Aunt Susanna was mixing cornbread. "There's just one thing," she said. "None of you must get sick again before we reach Oregon, because I haven't got a spot or a speck of medicine left!"

CHAPTER NINETEEN

LOSSES

The days passed, each one very much like the one before. On the evening of the day after the Indians had come, a strange noise could be heard as the travellers made their camp. As darkness fell sounds of far-away singing and shouting and whooping came to their ears from somewhere across the prairie. Some of the blood-curdling yells sent shivers down Ruth's back.

"It's the Cheyennes—we must be passing somewhere near their camp," said Uncle Seth, pushing back his cap and scratching his head.

"Are those war-cries?" wondered Aunt Susanna.

"I don't think so," said Uncle Seth reassuringly. "Since their visit yesterday I've got a new theory about all this singing and shouting. I'm wondering if maybe it's nothing to do with the warpath at all, but some sort of witch-doctor ceremony to try and cure the sick children. They do that sometimes."

But Ruth noticed that he kept his gun handy, and he and John did not go hunting but stayed close to camp. The noise went on at intervals all night, stopping sometimes and then starting up again. It was too far away to keep them awake, but Ruth woke often all the same and listened to that strange yelling and singing. Whether it was war-cries or witch-doctors, it was eerie and frightening, and everyone was glad when morning came and they could drive away from there.

They crossed a river and were coming to another patch of mountainous country. Uncle Seth was worried about wolves and bears and lynxes now that they were all on their own. Each night the cow and the horses were tethered close to the wagon, and he and John took it in turns to sit by the fire and keep watch. They missed the safety and security of the other wagons and men.

But in some ways travelling was easier than it had been, because the trail left by the rest of the caravan was fresh and could easily be followed. They could see where the pioneers had camped, by the ashes of their fires and the bones which the dogs had chewed and left behind.

At one camp they saw something which brought tears to all their eyes—a tiny, rough cross which stood some way back from the trail near a little mound covered with a pile of rocks and stones. They all got down and went slowly to look at it. There was a name carved on the cross, 'Anna Louisa Forester, aged five months', and the date. It was the little baby who had suffered so badly from earache.

Uncle Seth and John and David took off their caps and they all stood round the little grave with heads bowed. Ruth and Mary Rebecca sobbed, and under her sunbonnet tears were rolling down Aunt Susanna's cheeks. But she quickly tried to recover herself.

"Come, don't cry," she said. "The little one hasn't any pain now, and she is safe and happy with Jesus. We will do no good by grieving."

They turned and went back to the wagon. But all that day their hearts were heavy because of the little baby who had died. She would never see Oregon and grow up there.

That night they travelled on late because Uncle Seth wanted to get through the mountains and on to open ground again. Dusk was falling as they toiled up a slope, and everyone hoped that this was the last mountain ridge. John had climbed on ahead on foot, and he stood on the top of the rise outlined against the fading sky.

"It's all right," he called to them. "There's flat ground again once you get over this hill."

They reached the very top of the rise and stopped for a moment for everyone except Uncle Seth to get out. It would be a hard haul for the horses to get the wagon over the brow of the hill, and the wagon must be as light as possible. Belle and Benny were tired, their chestnut backs and sides were streaked with lather, but they strained their weary muscles for one last big effort. They pulled the wagon over the top and began to patiently plod down the other side. Aunt Susanna and the children followed on foot, glad to stretch their tired legs after sitting still for so long.

Then suddenly something happened. There was a shrill, screaming whinny; the wagon shuddered and jerked to a stop at a strange angle. Everyone rushed to see what had happened. Poor Belle's tired eyes had not seen a hole in the rocky ground, and she had stepped into it. Her weight and that of the wagon following downhill had thrown her forward, and she lay kicking and threshing with her hoof stuck fast. Benny was plunging and rearing in fright and was in danger of being pulled over too.

Uncle Seth jumped down and ran to quiet them. It took him and John a long time to calm them and cut Belle loose. She could not get up, but lay on her side sweating and snorting, her eyes rolling with pain and fear. Uncle Seth straightened up from examining her leg, and Ruth thought that she had never seen such a look of despair on his face. "I can't do anything," he said shortly. "The leg's broken."

Ruth realised with a stab of shock and dismay what this meant. It was impossible to do anything for a horse with a broken leg out here in this wilderness. Uncle Seth would have to shoot Belle. She cried out and tried to run forward to the poor, tormented horse, but Mary Rebecca caught her skirt and pulled her back. "We can't do anything," she said shakily.

Uncle Seth managed to move the wagon until it stood firmer and at a less crazily tilted angle. He unhitched Benny and led him away.

"Come, children," said Aunt Susanna. "Let's go back a little way and find Polly. She hasn't come up the hill yet."

She herded them back the way they had come and down to where Polly was tearing hungrily at the scrubby grass on the hill. Ruth tried to be brave, but a cry escaped her lips as a shot rang out. When they got back to the wagon everything was over, and with Benny's help the men had dragged poor Belle's body away out of sight among the rocks. Ruth would never see her again.

Soberly they went about their evening tasks. Everyone was sad because they had lost Belle, and because the Foresters had lost little Anna Louisa. For the first time Ruth wondered if going all this way to Oregon was really worth while.

No-one could eat much supper. Benny was unhappy and restless. He whinnied often and tossed his head on his picket rope. He missed Belle and sensed that she had gone for good.

Uncle Seth built a large fire that night. He said that scavengers would be attracted to the dead horse and they must be kept away.

"Father," said David suddenly, "without Belle, how

can we drive the wagon? Can Benny pull it alone?"

Uncle Seth shook his head. "No, son, it's far too heavy. This big wagon needs a team."

Ruth looked at him wide-eyed in alarm. She had not thought of how they were going to travel with only Benny. What would they do?

She looked at the faces of her uncle and aunt and cousins, serious in the firelight, and did not dare to ask. It seemed as though they had reached the end of the trail. They could not go on.

CHAPTER TWENTY

INDIAN PONY

Next morning after breakfast a council of war was held round the camp fire. Uncle Seth said that one of them must ride back to James Day's settlement by the river on Benny and tell him what had happened. Then perhaps he would lend horses so that they could all go back there. It looked as though they would have to settle down with the Day family and the others after all.

"Couldn't we buy a horse from Mr Day to replace Belle, so that we could go on," suggested John, but his father shook his head. "Day and the others have only two or three horses between them—I guess they're as precious as gold to them," he said.

"It'll be dangerous, riding back through hostile Indian territory alone," said Aunt Susanna quietly. "I don't like to think of one of you doing it, Seth."

"I know, but there's nothing else for it," said her husband. "We can't move backwards or forwards without another horse, and we can't stay here. We'll rest Benny for today so that he's fresh, and one of us will start first thing tomorrow."

"I'll go," said John eagerly. "Benny and I can outrun any Indians—not that we'll need to, of course," he added, seeing the look on his mother's face.

Aunt Susanna tried to look cheerful and began to clear away the remains of breakfast. "I wonder if there is any meat to be had here," she said, to change the subject. "The food supplies are getting a little low, and the salt pork is almost gone."

Ruth knew that this was true. Cornmeal and flour were getting lower and lower in the barrels, and the butter and cheese and bacon would not last so very much longer. Polly's milk supply had decreased because of so much travelling until it hardly provided enough for the little ones.

"We can buy more supplies once we're settled in Day's camp," said Uncle Seth cheerfully, picking up his gun. "And in the meantime I'll go and see if I can shoot something for our dinner."

He went off whistling, but Ruth knew that inwardly his heart must be breaking. It was dreadful to have to turn back after coming so far. She wished that there was still some way that they could go on to Oregon.

All the morning Ruth helped her aunt and cousin with the work. They washed clothes and she helped to iron them, and afterwards she played with the twins. Everyone tried to be cheerful, but in all their minds was the thought that tomorow John would have to ride off alone, a journey that would perhaps take two or three days. He would have to pass very near to that Indian camp on the prairie. Ruth remembered the singing and shouting and whooping they had heard, and shivered.

Uncle Seth did not come home until the middle of the afternoon, and when he did all he brought was one not-very-large prairie chicken. He flung it down in front of the wagon and said disgustedly, "The wild life all seem to be hiding today. That was all I could find. We won't get very fat on it!"

"Never mind, Seth," said Aunt Susanna soothingly. "That will make a nice stew for our supper, with some potatoes and onions."

Supper was early, because Uncle Seth said that they must all go to bed in good time as John must be on his way at the crack of dawn. After the meal they all sat round the fire and read in turn from the Bible, and the older ones prayed. Ruth had never prayed out aloud in front of people before, but suddenly she felt that she must. So in simple words she thanked God for His goodness to her, and asked that He would help them now in this time of need. Everyone said "Amen", and suddenly she felt that some of the fear and worry had rolled away from her heart. Of course God would always take care of them if they trusted and followed Him. That was all one really needed to do.

Just as she finished speaking there was a sudden low growl from Sam. He was standing stiffly, ears laid back, staring beyond the wagon towards the brow of the hill. Everyone looked to see what was the matter, and Ruth's heart seemed to miss a beat. A group of Indians on horses were outlined against the sky, looking down at them.

Uncle Seth spoke to Sam to calm him, and got to his feet. Everyone else got up too. The Indians rode down the slope towards them, faces as expressionless as ever. Ruth thought that she recognised some of them from the time before. She was sure that one of them was the husband of the Indian woman, the father of the little sick papoose. An awful thought came into her mind—if the Indian baby had died, like poor little Anna Louisa Forester, then surely they would blame Aunt Susanna's medicines. They might have come to kill them in revenge!

But the Indian's tomahawks remained in their belts and they had no guns with them. Ruth saw suddenly that one of them was leading a riderless horse, a sturdy little grey and white pinto pony with a long mane and tail. This man rode up to Uncle Seth and stopped. He spoke a word or two, pointed to Aunt Susanna, then to the baby's father, and cradled his arms in a rocking movement. Then he spoke again, pointed to the wagon and handed the halter of the pinto pony to Uncle Seth.

Ruth knew that it was a gift, and suddenly she wanted to give these strange brown men something in return. Her little Bible was still in her hand after reading it with her family. As the Indians began to turn their horses she ran forward, and reaching up quickly pressed it into the hand of the one who had led the pony. A flicker of something like surprise passed over his coppery-brown face, he looked keenly at Ruth and then at the book. Next moment, still holding it in his hand, he and the rest had all galloped up the hill and disappeared over its crest.

The little Indian horse turned its head to watch them go but it stood quietly in Uncle Seth's grasp and did not try to follow. Ruth let out her breath in a long sigh, feeling limp with relief. Once more the Indians had not harmed them.

Everyone was talking at once, gathering round Uncle Seth and the little pony and chattering with excitement and relief.

"Is he for us, Father?" David asked, reaching up to stroke the pony's soft nose.

His father nodded. "I guess he is," he said slowly.

"But why should the Indians give us a horse?" asked Mary Rebecca in puzzled tones.

"Oh, don't you see, 'Becca?" cried Ruth impatiently. "The little papoose and the others must have got well, and they're so grateful that they gave us this horse to replace Belle. Oh, it's so marvellous! Now John needn't ride back to the settlement—we can go on to Oregon!"

"Well, I'm sure we're very grateful," said Aunt

Susanna, smoothing down her skirt. "But how in the world did they know we'd lost a horse? That's what I can't understand."

"The Indians know more than perhaps we give them credit for," said Uncle Seth. "I daresay there have been eyes watching everything we do ever since we entered the Indian territory. Well, we surely are grateful to them. This really is an answer to prayer."

His eyes were sparkling and Ruth felt that her heart would burst with happiness. Her uncle looked down and hugged her with his free arm. "It was a good thought to give them your Bible, Ruthie. Pray God that one day they'll be able to read God's word for themselves," he said.

John was stroking the neck of the Indian pony. "D'you think he'll drive in a team, Father? He can't have been used to harness. He isn't very big, either."

"But I'll guarantee he's as strong as an ox—these Indian ponies are," said Uncle Seth. "As to driving in harness—well, there's only one way to find out."

They went at once to get Benny and hitch him up with the new horse. The grey-and-white pony was docile and did everything that was required of him. He and Benny quickly touched noses and made friends, and when harnessed to the wagon they pulled together smoothly.

"There's one thing about the Indians," said Uncle Seth as they unhitched them again. "They really love their horses and train them marvellously. This fellow can't have felt harness before and yet he takes to it like a duck to water."

The gift of the Indian pony really did seem like a miracle. They spent the rest of the evening discussing names for him. David wanted to call him Paint because he was a pinto pony. "That means painted pony—we learnt it in school," he said. It seemed a good name. The pony's grey markings did look as though they were painted on to his smooth, white hide.

"And I guess he's as smart as paint," said Ruth.

So it was decided, and just outside the circle of firelight Paint lifted his head and whinnied softly as though he approved of the new name.

CHAPTER TWENTY-ONE

PRAIRIE FIRE

With Paint and Benny pulling together in harness, Polly plodding behind, and Sam trotting in the shade beneath the wagon, the trek went on. All through August the weather was hotter than ever, with a blazing sun shining down all day on the hot, baked prairie. Uncle Seth said he had never seen such a summer.

In the wagon everyone suffered from the heat. Ruth and Mary Rebecca were sticky and perspiring in their long-sleeved, calico dresses, the twins' little faces were as red and shiny as apples and they continuously asked for drinks of water. Aunt Susanna fanned her hot face often, and John and David were stripped to the waist like Indians. All of them were as brown as berries from being so much in the sun and open air. Aunt Susanna said that the girls' complexions were probably ruined for life.

Ruth felt most sorry for the animals. The family could at least ride all day, but the animals had to walk mile after mile, day in and day out. Poor Polly had lost weight from travelling, her hooves were worn and her milk yield had gone down and down. No doubt she thought longingly of the farm in the East, with its cool meadows full of long, lush green grass. Sam trotted patiently all day, and all the time he panted loudly and perspiration dripped off his tongue in large drops. All he could see of the world was wagon wheels and hooves and the endless dust which they kicked up. Benny's sides were dark with sweat and streaked with lather. Only Paint seemed not to feel the heat too much. He pulled willingly all day long and seemed almost as fresh in the evening as he had when the day began.

Towards evening every eye would be eagerly straining for the first glimpse of some trees or bushes. Trees and bushes meant water, and water meant a place to stop and camp for the night. The best times were when they came to a big creek or a river. Then the animals would wallow in the water as soon as they were freed, and cool their tired hooves and drink their fill. Sometimes if the water was not too deep Aunt Susanna would let the children put on their oldest clothes and go in too. That was the very best time of the day, to be looked forward to all along the hot, dusty miles of travel.

Uncle Seth said that the weather must surely break soon. All the time they had been on the trail there had been only a very few spells of rain. The prairie grass was brown and dried-up. All the creeks were getting lower, and sometimes they came to a creek-bed which had dried up altogether.

One day they had to travel far into the evening before they could find a creek with water in it. When at last they came to one it was shallow and sluggish, just a narrow stream of muddy water between wide stretches of dried-up, cracked mud. But it was water.

Ruth had had a headache all day from the heat and from travelling. The air was still and oppressive, with not a breath of wind stirring.

"I declare the atmosphere is like an oven," said Aunt Susanna, taking off her sunbonnet and fanning herself with it.

"It feels a mite thundery to me," said Uncle Seth hopefully, as he unhitched the horses. "Perhaps we're in for a storm. The weather can't go on like this for much longer."

"I certainly hope it will not," sighed his wife.

Ruth and Mary Rebecca climbed stiffly down from the wagon. They looked longingly at the creek, muddy and shallow as it was. Perhaps Aunt Susanna would let them go in bathing later on. But first there were the chores to be done.

At supper no-one could eat much. The heat from the cooking fire was unbearable, so everyone took their plates and sat about on the edge of the creek. Ruth was surprised when suddenly a big cottontail rabbit bounded past her so near that she could have reached out and touched it. The next minute she had leaped to her feet in alarm as a shout came from John.

He was on his feet and pointing South in the direction the big cottontail had come from. Rolling across the prairie was a big, black cloud which started on the horizon but grew nearer as they watched.

"Fire!" said Uncle Seth. "The prairie's on fire!"

Everyone was galvanised into action. Nearer and nearer came the black cloud, and now flames could be seen and there was a rushing, roaring sound. The dry grass caught like tinder and the flames ran and spread and crackled. There was a choking smell of burning and smoke.

"The creek!" cried Aunt Susanna, herding the children together. "All of you—into the creek!"

She made them all wade into the muddy water. John and Uncle Seth had hitched up the horses and they drove the wagon into the deepest part they could find. Even then the water hardly came past the axles. Polly had already waded in, and Sam swam out and trod water, looking towards the oncoming fire and whining.

The hot, black cloud roared nearer. Aunt Susanna scooped mud and water and plastered the twins with it, and told David and the two girls to do the same. The black, squelchy mud felt warm and sticky on their skins. Heat could be felt coming in great waves from the fast-approaching fire. Their eyes watered and smarted from the stinging smoke.

Then Ruth saw the wild animals coming. Staring and panting they raced before the fire which threatened to engulf them. There were antelope, rabbits, mice running, frogs hopping, snakes slithering through the grass, birds flying through the hot air. Some plunged into the creek and swam, while others leaped across the narrow parts and raced on. All were united in fear of this common enemy.

The little ones were screaming in terror. Ruth felt the acrid smoke catch in her throat, making her cough. Her mind was in a whirl. She could no longer think straight. Mary Rebecca was plastering her own hair and Ruth's with black, sticky mud.

"Crouch down," she urged in a choking voice. They held hands and crouched low in the muddy water.

The fire was almost on them when another roar seemed to mingle with the roaring of the flames. There was a brilliant flash followed by a tremendous clap of thunder, and next moment they felt a fresh wetness on their muddy skins.

"Praise the Lord!" choked Aunt Susanna. "It's raining."

The fire kept coming even with the rain falling, but its fury seemed diminished. The flames reaching out towards the creek bank seemed to retreat, and died away with a hissing sound. There was more thunder and lightning, and more and more of the glorious, blessed rain.

Soaked to the skin and choking and spluttering, the Carey family watched from the creek until at last the battle was over. Defeated, the prairie fire fizzled out until it was just wisps of black smoke rising from black, charred earth.

Ruth's legs wobbled with relief as she stood up. She staggered and would have fallen had it not been for Mary Rebecca's hand. John was driving the horses and the wagon with sucking, squelching sounds towards the bank. Aunt Susanna and Uncle Seth, drenched and dripping with mud and each carrying a screaming child, were wading out of the creek and David was following. Uncle Seth had his free arm round Aunt Susanna's shoulder. Polly and Sam were there too. The fire had not harmed them.

The rain still streamed down as the bedraggled company climbed into wagon and tent to change their wet clothes. The rain had washed away most of the mud. Aunt Susanna made the children rub themselves down briskly before putting on dry clothes. Ruth shivered a little, thinking how strange it was to feel cold after being too hot for so long. Afterwards Uncle Seth asked them all to kneel while he thanked God for once more delivering them from danger.

All night long it rained and rained. Thunder roared and crackled overhead and every few minutes the darkness was lit by brilliant yellow and blue flashes. But the strong canvas cover did not let in a drop of rain, and Ruth was snug and warm and content as she lay in bed. Everyone was safe. The rain would refresh the parched ground, and the fire had not been allowed to touch any of them. God was truly caring for them. In spite of the thunder and lightning and the drumming rain, she slept soundly.

CHAPTER TWENTY-TWO

THE PROMISED LAND

In the morning the creek had risen and was flowing brown and swift almost up to the wheels of the wagon. Where the fire had not reached, the grass already showed greener and fresher, and there was a cool wind blowing. The hot weather had gone for good.

Travelling was easier now. By day the sun still shone warmly, but the nights were cool enough for everyone to be glad of the camp fire to sit around.

A week or two later Aunt Susanna took out and aired all the red flannel underwear which had been carefully stowed away in a box in the wagon, and made everyone change into it. Ruth thought it felt scratchy and uncomfortable at first, but she soon got used to it and found its warmth comforting. At the first opportunity she and Aunt Susanna and Mary Rebecca washed all the summer things and put them carefully away with lavender bags.

"We'll be in Oregon before we need them again," said Ruth happily.

"We've got a way to go yet," said Aunt Susanna, sounding unusually grim.

Ruth knew that she and Uncle Seth were becoming increasingly worried about the journey. It was getting on for the fall, and they still had to cross the vast Rocky Mountain ranges, which Uncle Seth said would be perhaps the most difficult part of the whole journey. Already there was a nip of frost on some nights, and before too long there might even be the first falls of snow. If real winter weather struck while they were still in the mountains they would be in serious trouble. And food supplies were running very low. So far there was plenty of meat to be had for the hunting, and sometimes fish and berries to help out, but this might change when the prairies were left behind. They pushed on with an even greater urgency, following the trail left by the other pioneers.

The day came at last when the prairies and plains were left behind. Now the way lay always up and down steep mountain slopes, across plateaus and through rocky gorges and passes. It was hard work for Benny and Paint and Polly, and their hooves split and wore down on the stony ground. As they climbed higher the temperature fell and game became scarcer. Wolves howled very near the camp every night, and the fire had to be kept blazing to keep them away.

One morning after they had camped in a narrow mountain pass Ruth awoke to find the ground covered with a thin powdering of snow.

"Shoes and stockings on, children," said Aunt Susanna as they began to dress. It was cold and they were glad of their shoes and warm woollen stockings knitted by Aunt Susanna back in the East. The twins were excited to see snow, and ran everywhere shouting and looking at the tracks they made. There were other tracks, too, near the camp, where little animals and some bigger ones had prowled during the night.

The snow melted away during the morning, but two nights later there was another fall. This time it took longer to go, and they drove through it, slipping and slithering a little sometimes. That day Uncle Seth could not manage to kill any game to eat. The days were growing shorter and it got dark soon after making camp, so there was not much time for hunting.

"We'll just have cornmeal mush for supper," Aunt

Susanna said in her usual cheerful way. "I'm afraid there'll be no milk, though—just enough for the little ones."

She served out a very small bowlful each, and though Ruth tried to make it last a long time it did not even seem to half fill her stomach. For the first time since she had lived with her aunt and uncle, she went to bed hungry.

Food now became the greatest anxiety. It was a rare day when a rabbit or a small mountain goat could be shot in these barren mountain ranges. There was just not time to hunt for food and to press on before winter came.

"Can we hold out, do you think, Susanna?" Uncle Seth sometimes asked, and Aunt Susanna always replied cheerfully, "Oh yes, I think so, Seth."

But the cornmeal and flour were almost gone. The bacon, salt pork, butter and cheese had long been finished, and there was not much milk to be had from Polly. When there was no meat they lived only on cornbread or mush and coffee, with sometimes some preserves from Aunt Susanna's dwindling supply.

"I think we could manage on just two meals a day," said Aunt Susanna one morning. "If we didn't have to stop at noon we'd make better time, wouldn't we?"

So now there was only breakfast and supper, and a long, long day of travelling in between. Thank goodness there was still some feed for the animals. It would have been awful if they had to pull all day on an empty stomach, thought Ruth.

But it was bad enough having empty stomachs themselves. Uncle Seth and Aunt Susanna sacrificed for the children and their cheeks began to look gaunt and thin. Everyone felt dull and listless and they were glad to go to sleep at night. Ruth felt that perhaps they would never get to Oregon but would just go travelling on and on through the mountains until they starved to death. She said so to Uncle Seth one evening, and he took her on his knee and reminded her of God's love for them, and how He had seen them through many dangers and trials already.

"Why, God has brought us almost to the very threshold of Oregon," he said. "He won't fail us now. Just remember the very first time you trusted Jesus, Ruthie, in that river bank hole, and you go right on trusting Him."

Ruth felt comforted. She knew that Jesus was her own Saviour, and that He loved her so much that the hairs of her head were all numbered. They would surely reach Oregon very soon.

But the day came when there was not a single crumb of cornmeal left. John squeezed out a small mug of milk for each of the twins, and the others had a cup of weak coffee with a little sugar. That was all. Hunger gnawed at Ruth's stomach as John hitched up Paint and Benny to the wagon. Standing beside it, she overheard her uncle and aunt talking in low tones so that the children would not hear.

"What happens now?" Aunt Susanna asked. "I don't think we can go far without food, Seth. Shall we have to kill the cow?"

Ruth almost cried out with horror, but clapped her hands over her mouth as she saw Uncle Seth shake his head. "Not today," he said, and looked up to where the next of the endless mountain ridges loomed before them. "We'll go just to the other side of that for today, and make camp early. Then John or I will take the gun and hunt until we get something. If we don't, then tomorrow——" He did not finish, but Ruth knew that tomorrow Polly might perhaps have to die.

As they began slowly to creak up the slope she felt almost numb with misery. It would be terrible if they had to kill and eat Polly, poor patient Polly who had followed them so faithfully and gladly given them all the milk she had. She felt that it would almost be better for them all to starve to death together than to do that.

She tried to pray as they toiled up the slope but somehow her thoughts were confused. The gnawing hunger in her stomach made her feel dull and stupid, and her head kept drooping on to Mary Rebecca's shoulder. Her cousin's arm went comfortingly around her and Ruth cuddled up gratefully to her. Mary Rebecca had been marvellous ever since the food ran short, never complaining and giving every crumb she could to the younger children. She was so kind that Ruth felt ashamed. She vowed that if ever they reached Oregon she would be much nicer to her than she had been in the past.

It was early afternoon and Ruth was dozing when at last they reached the top of the ridge. As the wagon stopped there was a shout from David which woke her with a start. She sat up sleepily. The twins still slept, but everyone else was crowding round the front of the wagon, staring downwards. What fresh calamity could have happened, she wondered dully.

Then she saw that every face was alight with joy. Rubbing her eyes she stumbled to the others and looked over their shoulders. For a moment she stared in disbelief, wondering if she could still be asleep and dreaming. Instead of another range of mountains, there was a beautiful valley stretching as far as the eye could see, with the afternoon sun shining on it and the grass still green. A river wound through it, and there were trees, still wearing their autumn colours of bronze and brown and yellow. Cows and horses grazed on the green grass, and far below them blue smoke curled up from a group of small log cabins.

Ruth hardly dared to speak for fear all this would suddenly vanish. "Uncle Seth," she said in a hoarse whisper, "is this—is this Oregon?"

Her uncle nodded and his gaunt face as he turned towards her was ablaze with joy. "Praise the Lord—it is Oregon," he said. "Those cabins may be the new homes of some of our party. We're there, Susanna, we're there!"

Aunt Susanna nodded without speaking and Ruth saw that there were tears of thankfulness on her cheeks. John and David and Mary Rebecca were gazing as if they could not see enough of that wonderful land. Even Sam had come from under the wagon and was whining eagerly as he looked down into the valley.

"Let us give thanks," said Uncle Seth. So everyone climbed down and knelt on the stony ground on the brow of the hill as he simply offered thanks to God for bringing them in safety to the promised land. Ruth's heart was full to overflowing with thankfulness. Here, there would be food and shelter and warmth and work to do. Here, men like Uncle Seth would serve their Lord and tell others of His love as they worked to make their country great. And here Ruth herself would grow up and do with her life whatever her Lord had planned for her.

When Uncle Seth had finished praying they remained kneeling for a while, offering their own silent prayers. Then, for the last time, they climbed back into the wagon and slowly drove down the hill into that beautiful green valley.